ESKIMO SUMMER

" The pans ride in and you have to anchor a couple
of miles off shore "

Eskimo Summer

By
DOUGLAS LEECHMAN

LONDON
MUSEUM PRESS LIMITED

First published in Great Britain in 1950

PRINTED IN GREAT BRITAIN BY
NORTHUMBERLAND PRESS LIMITED
GATESHEAD ON TYNE

For
RUTH

CONTENTS

Chapter		page
1	One-Eyed Bobby Says "Yes"	11
2	One Skin—Ten Dollars	24
3	The Dance in the Warehouse	35
4	We Leave for the Button Islands	44
5	An Eskimo Sealing Camp	60
6	Crossing Perilous Gray Straits	75
7	Our Camp on the Button Islands	86
8	Frozen Houses	103
9	The Second Igloo	117
10	Jenny's Cooking	131
11	The Conjuror's Platform	144
12	Back to Port Burwell—and Emily	160
13	Bobby Spends His Wages	173
14	Nunaingok—The Hidden Land	186
15	Bobby Goes Hunting Again	201
16	The Last Igloo	216
17	A Formal Visit	230
18	Last Days and Farewell	246
	Appendix	253

ILLUSTRATIONS

1 "The pans ride in and you have to anchor a couple of miles off shore . . *Frontispiece*

facing page

2 All the Eskimos in the district gather at the Post at ship time 16

3 "Ship day is a big event" . . . 17

4 "Here was another load of freight" . . 32

5 "Furs are never loaded till the last possible moment" 33

6 "All the girls had changed to their best clothes" 48

7 Port Burwell. The H.B.C. store carries a flag. No. 1 warehouse is opposite on the right . 49

8 The start of a kayak race . . . 64

9 "The Eskimos have amazingly fine teeth" . 65

10 "Soon another family arrived" . . . 80

11 "Not much care had been taken in the construction of the grave" . . . 81

12 "The watch for seals is constant and unremitting 96

13 "This is a land of very rapid run-off" . . 97

14 "Simmering over the soapstone koudlee or lamp" 112

15 "There are decided advantages to having two tents" 113

facing page

16 "No regular bedtime for Eskimo children" . 128

17 "Unaccustomed to petting and none too trustful
of any man" 129

18 "A bannock is a simple thing to cook" . . 144

19 "A much more carefully built igloo" . . 145

20 "It was the conjuror's platform" . . 160

21 "Duffle" or blanket cloth is used extensively
for clothing 161

22 "Tents are low down to the ground, reducing
wind resistance" 176

23 Eskimo children look surprisingly like Japanese
dolls 177

24 "We saw the smoke of the *Nascopie*" . . 208

25 "There was a large group of people waiting for
the *Nascopie*" 209

ACKNOWLEDGMENTS

*The illustrations, above, numbered 1, 3, 4, 5, 6, 9, 10, 13,
14, 16, 18, 22 are reproduced by courtesy of The National
Film Board; 7, 8, 17, 21, 23, 24 by courtesy of The Hudson's
Bay Company; 2 by courtesy of J. W. Anderson.*
The remaining six prints were supplied by the Author.

Chapter I

ONE-EYED BOBBY SAYS "YES"

IT'S a chancy business, is navigation, down North. One day, all is clear sailing; bergs and floes seem to steer clear of you intentionally and you bowl along without a care in the world; and then, the very next watch, a ship can hardly find room to turn her propeller over, so thickly does the ice press about her, bow and stern. One day, a harbour will be free and open; then, with a sudden perverse shift of wind, the pans ride in and you have to drop anchor a couple of miles off shore and wait for a change in the weather, or another tide, to send the ice running abroad; before you know it, the harbour is clear again, and in you go.

That's how things were when we sighted Port Burwell, on Killenek Island, at the far northern tip of the Labrador. Both the harbour, and the larger bay in which it is but a small cove, were solid with heavy pack-ice through which we could scarcely batter our way at all. For five tedious days the ship lay helpless, before we could work in close enough to begin landing cargo, poling and pushing the clumsy scows through the maze of pans and floes.

There were two possible ways of getting ashore: one, by scrambling over the rough ice, "copying" as the Newfoundlanders call it, from pan to pan for half a mile or so. Copying is an exciting and risky business, for the floating cakes of ice, close jammed though they are, rock and tilt as you leap from one to the other. Sometimes a change in balance, caused by the shifting of your weight, will tilt a pan so suddenly and violently that, before you can leap to the next, it will flip you off into the water. If you are lucky, there will be room for you to thresh about with arms and legs till you can climb up on top of the next pan; if not, the one you just left, relieved of its burden, will heave itself back into place, nipping you neatly between its own sharp edge and that of its neighbour. To my mind, copying is a method of travel best learned when young, and relinquished when older.

The other method of getting ashore—slower, safer, and more sedate—is to ride on one of the cargo scows. "Ride" is a misleading word though, for you must work your passage, pushing aside the ice which blocks every fathom of progress. If you have a boat-hook, you push with that, bracing yourself firmly against the cleats on the deck, straining and grunting, but producing no visible effect; if you have no boat-hook, you use your legs instead, lying with your chest on the low rail which surrounds the deck, your elbows notched inboard, your feet against the ice, still straining and grunting.

Slowly the pans move aside, reluctance evident in every inch, for each pan has to move its neighbour before it itself can move, and this one its neighbour in turn, till you are convinced, and not without reason, that you are moving every accursed pan in the harbour.

Nevertheless, this was the method I chose, for I ran less risk of a ducking and could keep an eye on my equipment during its transit from ship to shore.

This was my fourth visit to Port Burwell. The year before I had called in here three times while on a reconnaissance trip, and had selected this area and the Button Islands, which lie a few miles to the north, as two sites to be examined in detail.

Though the jump in the middle is a long one, Killenek

Island, the Button Islands, and Resolution Island, form stepping-stones by means of which one may cross the eastern end of Hudson Strait, and I felt that hereabouts might be found archæological evidence which would throw some light on the problems of Eskimo migrations in the Arctic, problems to which we, in the National Museum of Canada, have devoted a good deal of attention.

As far as the white man is concerned, Port Burwell was established in 1884, though there had been a native village near by for many years, perhaps centuries, before. In that year an expedition was sent north by the Canadian Government to study ice conditions and their effect upon navigation in Hudson Strait and Bay and a series of observation stations was established. The official report by Commander Gordon records the establishing of the station:

> On the shore of this harbour I selected a site for Observing Station No. 1, and named the place Port Burwell, after the observer appointed to that station. Two families of Eskimos were discovered about six miles distant from Port Burwell. The work of landing lumber and supplies was begun at once and by four o'clock on the afternoon of Friday the 8th [of August], the buildings were up and all was in readiness for departure. I placed Mr. H. W. Burwell [of London, Ontario] in charge of this station, with Messrs. Currie and Campbell as stationmen.

Burwell and his two assistants stayed there all through the following winter, making frequent observations of temperature, precipitation, barometric pressure, wind, and ice conditions and were relieved the following summer.

It was not until fourteen years later, in 1898, that a trading station was opened at Port Burwell, when Job Brothers, of Newfoundland, put up four wooden build-

ings, one of them a store, with Mr. Julius Lane in charge.
He lived in Port Burwell for many years, but during his
time the place was more often called Blandfort Station,
after a local sea captain, or Bishop Jones' Village.

The first resident missionary, the Rev. Mr. Stewart,
came about 1900 but, as he could not speak the native
language, he had but little effect on the people. In 1902,
Job Brothers offered the station for sale to the Moravian
Missions and the deal was completed in 1904. Then,
Mr. S. Waldmann, a Moravian missionary, replaced Mr.
Stewart, who went to Fort Chimo at the south end of
Ungava Bay.

The building of the large new mission house was begun
in 1905, but by the autumn of 1906 the walls were still not
up and only the stone foundation was completed. Waldmann had but little help and the Eskimos were quite
unfamiliar with such work. On the 15th of September,
1907, the building was sufficiently near completion for the
first religious service to be held between its walls.

In 1925 the Hudson's Bay Company took over all the
Moravian Mission's trading stores along the Labrador
coast, including Killinek, which they renamed Port Burwell, but the mission continued in operation without the
trading store until about 1928 when the last of the Moravian missionaries left the building, which still stands
empty and deserted.

Here I was, then, ashore with all my belongings and
equipment, prepared to stay till the Hudson's Bay Company's ship, R.M.S. *Nascopie*, should return in two
months' time on her way south again. How should I
fare? Whom could I get to work with me? How should
I get over to the Button Islands? And what might I find
there?

Seen from a distance, the shores surrounding the little
harbour are bleak and forbidding. The Land that God

gave Cain, it has been called, but there is no evidence that
Cain ever was able to make use of it. There are no trees
or bushes to soften the outlines of the rocky land and in
only a few places are the slopes and flats covered with
grass. The vegetation as a whole is buff-yellow or brown
in colour and green plants are scattered so sparingly that
they are quite insufficient to tint the desolate landscape
except in isolated patches.

Once one steps ashore, however, the picture is changed,
at least during the few brief weeks of summer. Then all
the flowering plants are in full bloom, hurrying along in
their desperate race to bud, flower, be fertilized, set their
seed, ripen it, and disperse it, before they are locked once
more in the rigid immobility of the long months of winter.
The more fertile, or more constantly watered, lowlands are
ablaze with colour; riotous masses of Arctic plants which
would drive a rock gardener to an ecstasy of mingled
delight and despair. Moss Campion and Stonecrop, glowing purple Fireweed, the yellow Arctic poppy, and many
others, all strive to show themselves to the best possible
advantage and, no matter how dwarfed by the cold and
inactivity of the greater part of the year, each individual
plant makes every effort to produce as many large and
brilliant flowers as possible, so that fertilization and,
hence, perpetuation may be assured.

So thickly spread, so colourful, are flowers in some
favoured areas that the newcomer literally hesitates in his
stride, searching for a barer spot where he may set down
his foot without crushing such delicate beauty out of
existence.

The Eskimo, naturally enough, is not restrained by any
such compunction. To him all these are merely plants,
their importance and interest in direct proportion to their
potential usefulness. If it bears leaves, or roots, or fruit
that may be eaten, if it provides tinder or lamp-wick, or

has some other definite value, a plant is given a name so
that one may speak about it and be understood. Otherwise it is just a plant and nobody but a foolish white man,
who is always asking senseless questions, would wonder
what its name might be.

However, I had not come ashore merely to admire the
flowers. My first task was to engage an Eskimo as a guide
and assistant and to make arrangements for transportation over to the Button Islands, for I had decided to
investigate them first, while fair weather might still be
expected. I explained my needs to Jackie Ford, a Hudson's Bay Company interpreter, and was immediately told
that One-Eyed Bobby was the very man I needed.

Bobby's first appearance was not very impressive. He
wore a dark green knitted tuque, a parka of heavy
blanket cloth which, once white, was now a dirty grey, a
pair of dark woollen trousers the bottoms of which he
had tucked into *kamiks* or sealskin boots, black in colour
and unprepossessing in looks, but of such wonderfully
tight sewing and sound workmanship as to be completely waterproof. Sealskin mitts protected his hands
from the wind which, even towards the end of July, was
chill and raw.

He stood about five and a half feet in height, well
and squarely built, with broad shoulders, a narrow waist,
shortish legs, small hands and feet. His skin, a light
brown, was warm and glowing, his cheeks slightly red-
der, and his face sadly marred by the loss of his left eye.
His remaining eye, deep brown, was quick and bright.
He carried himself easily and confidently, alertness and
competence were indicated by his every look and action.
Here, most undeniably, was a man.

Bobby listened quietly while the interpreter told him
what was wanted. We were sitting in the post manager's
office.

" All the Eskimos in the district gather at the Post at ship time "

"Ship day is a big event"

"How long would the white man want me to work for him?"

"Till the ship comes and goes for the last time this year."

Bobby's one eye shifted from Jackie Ford to me.

"Late summer is the time when I hunt caribou to get their skins to make clothes with," he said. "If I spend my time digging in the houses of the old people, I shall have no skins."

"True, but this man will pay you for your work; then you can buy caribou skins from other hunters who have more than they need, and you can buy warm woollen clothes from the Company's store here."

Bobby thought this over, and once again his eye was turned on me. One has to be so careful about white men, they are frequently quite helpless in the North country, and yet stubbornly insistent that everything must be done in their way. Undoubtedly also they are very rich and pay well for what they want.

"Very well," Bobby agreed. "We will go with the white man. When does he wish us to begin?"

"As soon as things can be made ready. His tents and other things are lying in Number One Warehouse now."

"But hold on a minute," I laughed when Bobby's decision was translated to me. "Why do you say 'they' will go with me? I need only one man."

"Yes, I know, but if you hire Bobby, you have to hire his whole family. You see, he can't just leave them here to fend for themselves. Somebody has to get meat for them, or they'll starve."

"Of course; but can't Bobby's brother—Mark, is it? Can't Mark do that?"

"Maybe he could, but it would be much better the other way, and won't cost any more. You see, you'll have both Bobby and Mark to help you with your work;

B

Lily, that's Bobby's wife, will do the cooking for the natives; his sister, Jenny, will look after you, because she's cooked for white men before; and little Jimmy, well, he's only four, so of course he'll have to go along too."

"Five altogether! It seems like a large party for a short season's work."

"But it's not really. It's just an ordinary Eskimo family, with you going along as a friend. Any year they might spend a week or two on the Buttons, though Bobby says he hadn't expected to be going there this year."

"All right, then! That's the way it shall be. But there are still things to be settled first."

One by one the details were arranged. My own equipment was to be carried on a motor-boat belonging to the Hudson's Bay Company. All Bobby's stuff—tent, bedding, clothes, tools, hunting gear and kayak—everything he owned almost, except his winter outfit, dogs and sled, would be loaded on his own sailboat and this would be towed by the motor-boat.

Then the matter of food supplies had to be discussed. How much flour, tea, sugar, lard, and baking powder would an Eskimo family of four adults and one child consume in six weeks? Could Bobby draw some of his prospective wages in advance? And, now this was an important detail, how much was the *kablunah* going to pay him?

Here's another vital thing! How are we going to get back from the Buttons? The crossing is a dangerous one and Bobby couldn't risk loading everything on his little sailboat, unless the weather was quite evidently set fair, which it seldom is in this part of the world.

"Speaking of the weather," I said to Jack Ford, "here is something I want you to explain to Bobby. Whenever

any question arises as to whether we should travel or stay
in camp, the final decision rests, not in my hands, but in
his. He knows this country and knows it well. He
knows when it is safe to travel and when it is not. Will
you tell him this? "

Bobby had been listening intently, though he couldn't
understand one word in a hundred. Now he turned ex-
pectantly to Jack.

"That is good," he nodded vigorously when he had
been told what I had said. "This white man is not a
fool like some of the others. I am glad that it has been
arranged so. Now I shall go to tell my people what has
been done."

Hardly was Bobby out of sight along the rocky trail
which led to his tent when we saw him returning in the
company of a girl.

"Here's Bobby coming back, and he's got Jenny with
him," commented Jack. "He must have met her on
the trail."

We had walked down the wooden sidewalk which
leads from the living quarters to the store, and sat down
on the front stoop to wait for them. When they got
closer, I could see Jenny peeking at the stranger who
had so suddenly been added to her family, but she did so
with short, quick glances, for she would not be so unman-
nerly and immodest as to stare openly.

She was short and, dressed as she was, somewhat
shapeless. She wore a brilliant plaid shawl over her
straight, black hair, a cotton blouse with no least preten-
sion to cut or style, an equally nondescript cotton skirt
with a printed flower pattern, much too thin to afford
any protection in such a climate. Under this, however,
the presence of other garments, numerous and warm,
was easy enough to divine. It is surprising that Eskimo
women, such skilful tailors when making fur clothing,

should be so awkward in handling cloths of the lighter weaves. Blanket cloth they use just as they would fur.

On her feet, Jenny wore sealskin *kamiks*, like those Bobby and everybody else wore, a little smaller, but just as efficient and serviceable.

The old native costume is seldom seen in this part of the country nowadays, for the people all get woollen things when they can, or cotton, or even rayon. Caribou skins used to be the correct thing for winter wear, and the woman's coat was a striking and beautiful garment, with a long tail hanging down at the back. In summer, working clothes of seal skins were more usual and, as a rule, attractive neither in appearance nor in smell.

Jenny cannot have been more than about twenty-five, but her dress gave no hint as to her figure; there was no suggestion of style, or grace, or even youthfulness about her. Yet she felt presentably dressed, for were not all her things bought at the white man's store? Had not her brother, Bobby, who was here with her now, traded many fine white pox pelts for what she was wearing? She had even rings and bead necklaces, and her shawl was almost new and quite clean.

"This is Jenny," said Jackie Ford, and Bobby grinned proudly.

Jenny put out her hand and so did Bobby. True, we had already shaken hands when first we met a couple of hours ago, but the Eskimos of the eastern Arctic like to shake hands on every possible occasion. Even the tiny ones, spread-eagled on their mothers' backs, will hold out a grimy little paw to meet the white man's hand. What matter whether it be the right or the left? Their mothers are always immensely pleased and amused when the *kablunah* politely takes the tiny hand.

I grinned cheerfully at Jenny and she answered with a pleasant smile. Her normal expression was rather

straight-faced, almost too serious, but her disposition
was equable and I never knew her to become angry or to
show any unpleasantness of temper during our weeks
together.

Another girl, whom I had already met and knew to
be the cook at the Company's living quarters, now joined
us. Tola, I was told her name was, which I later found
to be the Eskimo pronunciation of Dora. She is Jenny's
sister and had for some time, if not always, been lame.
Now she learned that Bobby's family had adopted me
for the summer.

After a brief discussion with Jenny, Tola led me into
the store, pointed to my boots, and asked me something
in Eskimo. I looked blank, and turned to Jackie Ford.

"She wants to know if you have any *kamiks*," he explained. "You'll need them, all right, if you haven't."

"No," I admitted. "I'd expected the women could
make me some later."

"Much better get them now," he advised. "There's
a big stock of them in the store here, a whole winter's
sewing, so you'll be sure to get some that will fit."

Tola and Jenny had not waited for my decision to be
announced. Already they were diving into the deep,
large bin under the counter in which the sealskin boots
were kept.

"Let me see your foot," said Jenny, pointing. This
time I guessed what was meant easily enough, and stuck
my foot up on the edge of the counter while she and
Tola inspected it. Both girls broke into shrill giggles.

"They can never believe that white men have such
big feet," laughed Jackie. "All the people have small
hands and feet."

Quickly the two girls went through the stock of boots,
flinging all but the large ones back to oblivion in the
bin they had just come out of. Finally about a dozen

pairs were left. These they examined carefully, inspecting the sewing of the seams and testing the thickness of the soles. Some they rejected with lively comments and ridicule.

"They know exactly which woman made every pair," said Jackie. "They think some of the work is pretty poor. The boots are not made for their own use, so the women don't care much whether they are watertight or not. The girls will see that they get good ones for you, though."

At last five pairs were selected as being fit to wear. I tried them on. To my dismay, they were all much too big. Evidently the girls' impression of the size of my feet had misled them.

"No," said Jack, when I suggested this. "That's all right. They've got to be big. You've got another pair of socks to go inside, and then an even heavier pair made of duffle as well. The soles are so soft and thin that you couldn't walk in them else."

So the next thing was to have blanket cloth socks made and this job fell to Tola's lot for she had more spare time on her hands than had Jenny, who wanted to get back to her tent so that she could begin her preparations for our trip, and the socks had to be made at once, for there was no knowing how soon we might be able to get away.

With a piece of string, Tola measured the inside length of my foot from the big toe to the heel, and here she tied a knot; then the length from the top of the instep to the end of the big toe, and another knot; last of all, she measured across my instep from the floor, over, and down to the floor again. One last knot, and that was all.

That same afternoon she handed me two pairs of new blanket cloth socks which fitted to perfection. They were perfectly white, or with just a suspicion of cream colour, and reached up to a point just below my knees. Round the top they were decorated with embroidery in coloured worsted, both inside and out, though only the outside showed when they were being worn. Furthermore there was embroidery on the instep which would never by any chance be seen at all as long as I wore *kamiks* or my usual boots, or even slippers.

Now once more I could try on the sealskin boots and in a few minutes I had selected two pairs which fitted well, neither so short that they cramped my toes, nor so long that they were too loose. I wore them for the rest of the summer, on dry land, in wet grass, in swamp, in freshwater streams, and in salt water, and they never did leak a drop.

One thing my *kamiks* still lacked, and that was the braided cord of caribou sinew which runs through the hem at the top to tie them fast below the knee. This I pointed out to Bobby, and held up four fingers to show that I needed four such cords.

"*Sittamut*," said Bobby, nodding and smiling, and he in his turn held up four fingers. It was my first formal lesson in Eskimo, a language of which I then knew but a dozen words. I had feared we might have some trouble with the language problem, but actually things went very well. I soon picked up enough of it to express the more urgent thoughts, though mine must have been a strange gibberish indeed. However, Bobby and the others soon got to understand what I was trying to say and after a little while, even rudimentary conversations became possible. Never was there any serious difficulty, though there were many occasions on which I could not even attempt to say what was in my mind. More than once, I fear, I said what I most certainly did not mean.

Chapter II

ONE SKIN—TEN DOLLARS

IT is generally towards the end of July before R.M.S. *Nascopie,* supply ship of the Hudson's Bay Company, pays her first annual visit to Port Burwell, or one should rather say it was, for the Post is closed now. In some years she used to call there three times, in others once or twice only. All the Eskimos in the district knew when she was expected and gathered at the Post in anticipation of her arrival.

A day or so before she was due, little groups of people would climb to the lookout point on the top of a near-by hill. Here they would stand or sit, perhaps with a telescope, and gaze out over the sea where the stately icebergs drifted slowly with the tide. At last their patience would be rewarded and they would see a distant, low-lying streamer of light brown smoke, marking the presence of a ship. True enough, it might be merely a freighter, Churchill bound, in which case she would carry on steadily to the westward and vanish from their sight. But if it should really be the *Nascopie,* she would turn her bows to the southward after rounding the north-west corner of Killinek Island and, growing larger and larger, force her way through the pack-ice till she lay in the little harbour.

In shape, this harbour bears a rough resemblance to a capital "T." At the west end of the cross-bar stand the old buildings of the Moravian Mission, sad red on a

24

stone foundation, now desolate and abandoned. At the other end, lying snug in "Happy Valley," were the H.B.C. Post and the buildings of the Royal Canadian Mounted Police, now empty or torn down. In the main, upright stem of the "T," the ship lies at anchor and, on shore, right opposite her bows, where the stem and cross-bar of the "T" join, are the tents of the natives, clustered about a little brook from which the people get their drinking water.

Ship day is a big event for the Eskimos as well as for the whites. There may be old friends on the ship with whom to exchange the news of the past twelvemonth. Certainly there will be new people to see and to wonder about; there will be Mounted Police officers in their bright scarlet dress tunics; there will be Hudson's Bay Company officials wearing their peaked caps with the much-coveted badges in front; perhaps there will be new missionaries; and, quite possibly, there will be other white men and women who seem to have nothing to do but to wander all over the camp, peering curiously into the Eskimos' tents, pushing brazenly into the few white residents' houses as though they were hotels, buying curios in the store or direct from the natives, taking pictures, distributing cigarettes to the elders and tossing candy to the children for them to scramble for. To the Eskimo, the tourist is, on the one hand, an insoluble mystery; on the other, a somewhat pathetic figure, a joke, the embodiment of the senseless occupations and the helplessness of the *kablunah.*

There will be work to do, too; work for which one is paid, of course, usually in trade. There will be almost endless boxes, bales, crates, drums, sacks, cartons, and miscellaneous packages to be unloaded from the two big motor-scows which accompany the ship and are used to ferry cargo from ship to shore. All this stuff has to be carried along the little wharf and into the warehouse, some of it placed here and some there, but every single piece, without exception, must pass before the eyes of one of the white men from the ship, so that he can mark it on the long white paper which flutters in his hand.

Everybody joins in this work; men, young or old, even mere boys; women, some carrying babies on their backs, and some without, young girls and their grandmothers; even the cripples carry what they can. And when there is a pause, when the scows have gone for another load and the crew on the ship stop for something to eat, the Eskimos have a rest too. A fire is lit on the beach and a large kettle of tea is slung over it, a huge kettle into which endless white enamel mugs, each holding a pint, can be dipped without fear of its running dry. Near by stands a whole pailful of butter, or something which looks very like it, and near by, quite literally hundreds of ship's biscuits, hard as wood, all just waiting to be eaten.

This is a "mug-up." It's a grand feed. Everybody digs in, munching the hard-tack with powerful jaws, for Eskimos are blessed with most magnificent teeth. Now and then some tiny child on its mother's back reaches forward for a share of the good things she is eating and, with a little coo of affection she turns her face to the child's and transfers to its mouth the half-chewed cud in hers. Older children, able to look after themselves, are getting their full share, and why shouldn't they? Haven't they been working just as hard?

The smallest ones of all, too young even for semi-solid food, stay quietly on their mothers' backs till it is time to nurse them. Then the shawl is loosened, the woman stands up and, with a sudden alarmingly precipitous forward swoop, she spills the infant neatly out over her shoulder into her arms. Seating herself again, she bares her breast and offers it to the little one. Sucking busily away, the child's black eyes rove over the crowd of noisily chattering people, so surprising a scene for a little baby who hitherto has spent all its life in the family group.

Infants have to be removed hurriedly from their mothers' backs for other reasons than nursing, and the same technique is employed, usually only just in time. Many an inexperienced Eskimo mother has been most thoroughly drenched as a result of failing to recognize storm warnings.

It's nearly always time for a mug-up down North. If the tide happens to be against us, and we have to wait till it turns, out with the Primus, heat some water, and we'll have a mug-up. If it starts to rain heavily, and we have to lie in the lee of a cliff or take shelter in a cave— mug-up. If one of the dogs has run off on some errand of his own and somebody has to go after him, the others have a mug-up while waiting. If we shoot a polar bear and he is being flayed and dressed, a mug-up is indicated. Tea, hot, steaming, and always very welcome, and whatever there is handy to eat, is a mug-up, whether it be morning, noon, or the shivering middle of the night. It is the northern equivalent of a breather, a quick one, a cocktail. It is a social occasion, a welcome relief from tension, a boon to all men.

But here was another load of freight, and everybody got to work again, talking and laughing, tugging and hauling, slipping, scrambling, sweating, till everything on the wharf was safely tucked away in the warehouse. At last, when all the cargo destined for this Post had been unloaded, the tourists had taken their last photographs and bought the few remaining kayak models, and the cargo scows had been hoisted on deck, the ship left again with a farewell blast of her siren. The post manager breathed a sigh of relief, for now he could settle down to work, read his annual batch of mail and resume command of his domain. He had been glad to see the ship come, true enough, mighty glad; but he was more than glad to see her sail away again.

This was by no means the end of things for the Eskimos, though. Now they could really get to work! The first thing to do was to get some of the stuff out of the warehouse, in which it had hastily been piled almost any old way, and into the store where long-empty shelves awaited the new supply of riches from " outside."

For weeks now the Post had been out of this and out of that. No more sugar, perhaps, or no more tea. All the duffle cloth was sold, and there was no more of the brightly coloured silk and wool braid. The post manager selected this box and these bales, and they were carried across the little stream which flows down Happy Valley to the sea and up the other side to the store. Here a little group was seated on the wooden stoop outside the front door, speculating as to what might be in all these mysterious packages.

The post manager's clerk got to work and opened them up. It was his first year in the North, almost his first day, in fact, and he didn't know very much yet. The goods were taken out of the boxes and piled up on the counter, where they would be close at hand when they were to be transferred to the shelves.

"All right, Harry," the post manager called. "Don't put out more than a dozen of those red shirts. Just leave the others in the carton, and put it in the back room."

"O.K. What about these mouth-organs? Put them all out? "

"No, just the big ones. We'll sell them off first and then bring out the cheaper ones when those are all sold."

"O.K.," agreed Harry, learning his first easy lesson in merchandising.

"What's in this barrel? Apples! By all that's holy. I haven't tasted an apple for months."

Quickly he filled an empty carton and handed it to Tola who was standing by, waiting for supplies to take up to her kitchen.

"Here you are, Tola. Apples! Can you make apple pie?"

"*Marrik!*" answered Tola, meaning roughly "And how!" Smiling with pleasure, she limped off with the apples.

When all the things needed at the moment had been unpacked, and the reserves stored away in the attic or in the back room; when all the stuff for the Mounties had been taken up to their buildings on the south side of Happy Valley, opposite the Hudson's Bay Company's house, things began to settle down. At last every box had reached its destination, and the "Arctic wheelbarrows," wooden stretchers on which things too heavy for one man are carried, were put back in the corner of the warehouse where they belonged. It was time for another mug-up.

There was, after this mug-up, an air of quiet expectancy in the air. Soon, somebody would ask the post manager if he were ready to trade. Until to-day the store had been half empty, and there was little or nothing to trade for. But now——!

For a moment the post manager looked surprised, as if such an idea had never occurred to him.

"Trade?" he repeated, and glanced about the store. "Why, yes, I guess so," and he slipped automatically behind the counter. There was a little rustle of interest and pleasure from the group sitting outside, and several of them got up and came in.

The man who first asked to trade and his wife stood at the counter. In his hand he held an old sack, plumply filled, but not at all heavy. He undid the neck of the sack and shook out a single white fox skin, sleek, gleaming. The dry hide, scraped thin and clean till it was like parchment, crackled slightly.

The trader picked it up by the head and gave it a sharp snap to shake the fur into place, like a cat killing a mouse with a jerk of its head. He smoothed it down with his hand to test its softness and laid it on the counter to see its length. It was a prime skin. Both men knew that, the trader and the Eskimo. One skin—ten dollars.

The chips were laid out on the counter and the Eskimo was satisfied, for he could actually *see* his ten dollars, visible and tangible before him, not mere figures in a book. First he wanted cigarettes, one dollar's worth. The little packages were handed to him, and one of the chips taken from his pile. One chip—one dollar. At once he got out a cigarette and lit up. The thin blue coil of smoke rose from the tip of it and he inhaled deeply, held the smoke, and then slowly and luxuriously blew it out again. It was a long time since he had had a smoke. Meanwhile, his wife suggested that there were things needed in the tent. He nodded his agreement and, turning again to the trader, said that the woman would know what was wanted.

There was tea, and flour, and lard, and sugar to be thought of, as well as some tobacco for her too. These were placed on the counter before her and she put them in her shawl which she took from her head. The little pile of chips diminished quickly.

Now the man came forward again. He must have ammunition, at least forty rounds, ·303 British, but there were not chips enough left. His little pile of ten had gone, one by one, and there were still things he wanted to buy.

Once again he untied his flour sack and pulled out

another skin. Again the trader smoothed its fur with a shake. With pursed lips, he blew steadily on the back of the pelt and the soft hairs parted, down to their roots, revealing their length and gloss and the purity of their colour. Another prime skin—another ten dollars—another little pile of ten chips to be traded away one by one. The rest of the ammunition had to be paid for, some cloth for his wife to make a dress with and, for him, one of those warm red woollen shirts the clerk had just put up on the shelf there.

To the Eskimos, these shelves were an endless source of interest. To the visiting white man, there was in them a surprisingly close counterpart of any small country store. One side was devoted, in the main, to groceries; the other to dry goods. In the back was hardware. Hanging from the ceiling cross-beams was the usual medley of lanterns, pails, kettles, oilskins, rubber boots, traps, and other things which could be hung up.

Here and there on the counters, one of which ran almost the whole length of the store on each side, were small glass cases containing cheap jewellery, mouth-organs, Jews' harps, cakes of scented soap, powder compacts, and other small objects, attractively displayed and very sure to catch an Eskimo buyer's eye. Small racks held such things as bead necklaces and pendants.

Larger stands, in the corner, held rifles and an occasional shot-gun and, stacked in pyramids near by, were boxes of ammunition, seeming to promise success for the fortunate purchaser. Saws, hammers, brace-and-bit sets, appealed to the woodworking instinct of the natives who are almost all clever mechanics.

Pervading the whole store was the familiar mixture of odours: cheese, rope, brown sugar, coffee, soap, oil, new clothes, bolts of printed cottons, each contributed its share, and together they produced a combined smell which flooded me with a wave of nostalgia, for it was exactly the smell of a country store in a little village where I once spent a summer holiday, many years ago. Would I ever enter that store again, I wondered.

Now came Bobby's turn to do some trading. Already he was a marked man. Was he not taking the new white man with him this summer to show him where the Tunnits lived, many years ago? He didn't need to produce fox skins to trade with. In the first place, he already had a balance to his credit; in the second, he was assured of a good summer's wages.

This was almost "big business." Bobby wanted to get all the necessary supplies for his family of five for at least a month. Perhaps he'd better make it six weeks, just in case the weather delayed us, and so as to be on the safe side. The standard ration list includes flour, baking powder, lard, sugar, molasses, tea and so on, but Bobby wanted more than this. The molasses he would not have at all, but more sugar instead. Then, too, he wanted tobacco, and much ammunition, and needles and thread for the women.

"Wait," said Bobby. "What do I know of such things? Jenny is coming and with her, Lily, my wife. Let them have what they need."

Lily and Jenny could be seen on the brow of the hill, coming along the trail from the little cove south of the harbour, where Bobby had his tent.

The women approached slowly, for the trail was rough and narrow, and they walked carefully in their soft-soled boots. Their bright plaid shawls fluttered in the breeze and their skirts suddenly blew out sideways as they stepped into the current of air sliding down Happy Valley to the sea. They crossed the little brook by the wooden plank bridge and then climbed up the other side to the store.

" Here was another load of freight "

" Furs are never loaded till the last possible moment "

Lily was by no means beautiful. Seldom, indeed, can a name have been less appropriate. By some strange coincidence she, like her husband, had lost one eye, her right. How she lost it, I never discovered, for my command of her language was never enough for me to ask her about it or to have understood her explanation if I had. Bobby, I knew, had lost his when a cap exploded as he was loading rifle shells.

Lily was short and stocky in build and, though dressed much as Jenny was, by no means so clean. Her hair, straight, long, and black, was less frequently combed, her hands not so often washed, and she was much less active and intelligent than was Jenny. The loss of her eye handicapped her and she had difficulty even with the remaining one, for she could see but little with it. Sewing was tiresome for her and cooking, even in the ultra-simplified form customary with her people, too much of a nuisance to hold her interest. She much preferred to sit still on the blankets at the back of the tent and smoke quietly, occasionally pushing a bit of wood into the home-made stove.

For a moment, the prospect of being able to buy anything she wanted roused her and she went at once to the pile of plaid shawls on the dry-goods counter. Her fingers ran down them one by one, but she didn't venture to disturb them for she knew they would all have to be refolded and the trader would be angry. She could see them well enough as they were. Here was a vivid pink, here a screaming green, each liberally mixed with half a dozen other colours. It was a very difficult decision, but at last she picked out a brilliant and handsome blue with an intricate pattern running through it. Then she lost all interest. Anything else might mean work! Why buy yards of cotton print if you have to make it up into dresses. Let Jenny buy some; she's so good at sewing.

c

Lily shuffled out to the front stoop, sat down, propped her back against the wall of the store and rolled herself a cigarette, making some casual explanatory remark to Bobby as she settled down to rest. Jenny would look after everything.

Chapter III

THE DANCE IN THE WAREHOUSE

THE warehouse was a scene of great activity that night. A good deal of the stuff recently unloaded from the *Nascopie* had been put in here, but it was not yet arranged in its final position. Half a dozen men were busy stacking boxes, crates, and bales along the walls, leaving a large clear space in the middle and so disposing of the various objects that there was a row of single boxes in front, thus making a line of convenient seats.

At one end of the building, near a window, stood the fur press, a large structure of heavy wooden beams used for keeping bundles of fur under pressure while they were being made up into bales, sewn into strong Hessian cloth, laced with a special coloured cord made for the Hudson's Bay Company, stencilled and sealed. Often light enough to be carried by one man, many a fur bale is nevertheless worth several thousands of dollars on the London market at the fur auctions.

At the other end of the warehouse was the carpenter's shop, a partitioned-off space of perhaps seven by ten feet, with a work-bench running down the outer wall, lighted by two windows. Here were to be seen pots of paint, coils of wire and balls of cord, all the thousand and one odds and ends which gather in such places. On heavy nails in the upright two by fours hung a spare propeller for the motor-boat, steel traps, binder twine, short ends of rope, and, on the floor in the corner, a tin of linseed oil, turpentine, and kegs of nails.

At the narrow end of the warehouse, where the carpenter's shop took a bite out of it, was a stack of fur bales waiting to be loaded on the *Nascopie* on her last call before leaving for outside. Furs are never loaded till the last possible moment, for to do so is to increase the chance of losing them. The top of this pile of fur bales was a favourite retreat of the youngsters. Here they could lie flat on their bellies and gaze down on their elders below. Here was a fine chance for lots of giggling and fun if they could get the girls up there too. Sometimes they were successful in this, and sometimes they were not.

In this same warehouse, when I was there the year before, before I had met One-eyed Bobby, strange things had taken place. All the Eskimos in Killinek, and from far around, were gathered to see some pictures the white men had brought with them on the ship. Not just ordinary pictures, like those in books, but much larger pictures on a big white sheet, and even while one looked at them the pictures moved. Nobody had ever seen such a thing before, or even heard of it.

The people had been told in advance that a machine would make the pictures, so they came at the appointed time and took their seats on the floor, for that is where they were accustomed to sitting and, of course, there were no seats for the audience anyway. When the operator came in to start the show he found his guests all sitting with their backs to the screen and their expectant eyes fixed on the projector. After all, if this was the machine which made the pictures move, what was more natural than to sit so that one could watch it?

There was no doubt that the show had been a success, once the audience was re-oriented, though there were some parts of it that had left them considerably puzzled.

One film showed the ceremonial side of the life of King George V. None of it had meant much to the Eskimos, who had never in their lives seen such things as horses or carriages; trains, motor-cars and soldiers were equally unfamiliar and the whole thing was, to them, a series of pictures of totally strange things being done by unknown people in a peculiar country.

The next film, made in the Arctic, was another matter altogether. Here were things, and activities, and people who were quite familiar. Here, for instance, of all commonplace and comprehensible things, was an ordinary husky dog, such as everybody in the audience had in his own home and, when that dog rose to his feet, yawned, and walked off the screen, there was a howl of amusement and appreciation.

But what was this? Here were two men who had been known personally to some of those in the audience, and it was common knowledge that they were dead, for the news of it had been brought when the ship came in the year before. And yet, here they were, walking about on that white sheet in Number One Warehouse and doing the things that any living man might be expected to do. It was very strange and a little disquieting. Perhaps there was some truth in what the old people said about the magical little black boxes in which the white man could capture your soul and stick it down on a bit of shiny white paper.

Then came Mickey Mouse and at once all fears and doubts were dispelled. Immediately he was recognized and hailed with shouts of joy, but not as a mouse—as a lemming. And such an ingenious and daring little lemming, full of resource and courage, who could turn his own tail into a brace and bit and bore holes in the bottom of the boat in which his enemies were carrying him off. This was too much for one old woman, and she went off into such a series of high-pitched, wheezing shrieks and screeches of gasping, choking laughter that even her own family, accustomed to her habits though they were, thought she really was hysterical this time and dragged her, protesting, out into the open air.

After the show, there had been fireworks, more of the white man's magic, but all that was last year. This year there were no fireworks and no moving pictures, just an open space in the middle of the warehouse floor, a smoky lantern hanging from a convenient brace, and a mournful-looking young Eskimo girl fingering an accordion.

By now the people were gathering in some numbers. All the girls had changed to the best and cleanest clothes and had washed and beautified themselves for the occasion. Their hair was combed and braided and their parkas, if they wore any, were clean and white, of heavy duffle decorated with embroidery in coloured worsted or with strips of bright braid. Nearly all of them were wearing sealskin *kamiks*, but one or two girls actually had on silk stockings and shoes with medium high heels. This was a form of footgear which they considered most fashionable though very uncomfortable, especially on the rocky, narrow trails which led from their tents to the Post.

Bobby took me over to the far side of the warehouse and presented his brother, Mark. He was a strongly built lad of about twenty, with clear, bright eyes and an intelligent expression. Mark shook hands, smiling broadly, and said *"Aksunai!"* the usual form of greeting here, meaning approximately "Be strong, will you not?"

"Aksunai!" I answered. Mark looked like a most useful addition to the expedition.

Seated beside him was an Eskimo girl of about eighteen, prettier than many of them, clean and neat, smiling and obviously proud to be with Mark. She was introduced as

Emily, and Mark, quite evidently, considered her his personal property.

Fifty or more Eskimos were now grouped here and there, sitting on the rows of boxes and bales along the walls, some on flour sacks, others on tea chests, one or two on a big bale of sealskin boots, and others on the floor. Suddenly an accordion broke into a dance tune, but with no apparent effect, for everybody was absorbed in conversation and busy with the rolling of cigarettes. Everybody smokes as a matter of course, even quite young children. No refreshments were in sight, however; no sign of a mug-up!

The girl who was playing the accordion had a naturally sad expression, her long narrow face broke but seldom into a smile and, dexterous player though she was, she seemed never to enjoy her own playing, or to play at all except as a rather tiresome social duty.

The original Eskimo instrument of music was the drum and they had no other, except for a rudimentary whistle in the western Arctic, but to-day many of them have mouth organs and accordions which they play with considerable skill. A few of them have made crude violins from old boxes with braided sinew for strings, but there are notably not "musical" instruments.

Half a dozen white men were at the dance as well as the Eskimos. There was the post manager and his clerk, two Mounties, Jackie Ford and myself and we all took part in the dancing with just as much enthusiasm as anybody else.

There was no hope of seeing any truly native dances or of hearing any native melodies; these have all been done away with, officially at least, since the missionaries hold that it is sinful for their converts to indulge in such pagan practices. Instead the people dance square dances introduced by Scottish whalers, years ago, and the tunes they dance to are largely from the same source. More recently they have picked up melodies from the radio, an instrument which, since there is no man-made interference in the North, works exceedingly well.

A Roman Catholic missionary, when the radio was first introduced to his mission, was asked by the Eskimo what it was. He answered by giving it a native name meaning "that to which one listens." Later he learned that the Eskimos at Aklavik, hundreds of miles to the north-west of his station, had also given the radio a name. Theirs meant "that to which one listens *at will*," a subtle change effected by inserting a single syllable. The fact that one could turn the thing off when it became a nuisance evidently impressed the not-so-primitive natives.

Soon the men rose to their feet and strolled nonchalantly over to the groups of girls, selected their partners and took their places on the floor for a square dance. Eight couples made up the two sets for which there was room and one heard cries of "Two more couples wanted!" or whatever it might be, in Eskimo or English.

At last all was in readiness and the music, which had been going on rather half-heartedly all this time, took on a new vigour.

"*Taima!*" shouted somebody, meaning "Enough!" or "That's all!" and suddenly the dance, so long in starting, was under way.

"All join hands and circle right! Swing your partners! A la main left! Dos-a-dos!" All the well-known calls and figures were gone through and all with a wild enthusiasm and energy. The girls, it is true, tried to behave with the decorum expected of them and, though they might occasionally glance up to meet the eyes of the men dancing opposite them, usually they were straight-faced and downcast of eye.

Not so the men. They stared openly at their opposite

numbers, did all they could to make them laugh or smile, performing unexpectedly tricky steps and *pas-seuls,* breaking into short, shrill cries as do the Highlanders, "laughing like loons" as Jackie Ford commented.

Whether they were theoretically resting while the opposite couple was performing a figure or whether they themselves were actively engaged in it, the men "tapped" or "stepped" through the whole dance, beating time vigorously and accurately with their soft-soled sealskin boots in an impelling, drum-like rhythm. There was the soft scrape of the skin soles on the wooden floor, and the thick thudding of their heels, and it set up a pulsing, throbbing beat that insisted that everybody dance—dance till the end, dance till they drip and sweat and drop from exhaustion.

Jack Ford had suggested that I ask Tola for the first dance.

"She dances well, even if she is a little lame, and she'll teach you how," he assured me.

Tola was willing enough and soon I was in the thick of it. It was hot, hard, fast work but, once the fundamentals were grasped, not at all complicated. The grand chain brought me one Eskimo girl after another, all pleased to have the new white man dancing with them, all anxious to save him from making any mistakes.

It was a place of strong and penetrating smells, that warehouse. There was cheap perfume, and strongly scented soap, there was rancid seal-oil, and human sweat, the indefinable sharp and acrid smell of small children, none too clean, and the odours of the furs in the bales and the goods in the boxes all about us. There was colour, too, and movement, life and happiness. It was a most wonderful dance.

Faster and faster went the music, limited only by the dexterity of the sad-faced girl in twiddling her fingers on the keys. Louder and louder grew the shuffling, stamping rhythm when, suddenly——

"*Taima!*"

Abruptly the music stopped, the men led their partners back to their seats and, just as quickly, ran to the wide-open door for a breath of fresh air and a cigarette.

The girls, true to the habits of their sex, slipped off behind the warehouse in twos and threes to powder their noses, turning by some unwritten law to the left. Any of the boys who wanted to wash their hands, as most of them did, turned to the right, thereby arriving at the back of the same building. An excellent arrangement, affording unlimited scope for chatting *tête-à-tête* and little strolls in the near-by, shadowy hills.

It is at the dances that many of the boys get their chance for a few minutes with some girl who has been out of their sight for months. Their respective families may have been hunting in different areas and it is only the lure of ship time that has brought them together. Many a romance and many a marriage have resulted from a dance in Number One Warehouse.

The night air was cool and refreshing, and it was still far from dark at ten o'clock. The stars, though visible, were not yet brilliant, and the Northern Lights were beginning to glow and flicker over the hills to the north. Down in the cove could be heard the sob and rustle of the incoming tide and a slow breeze from the open sea carried the salty tang of seaweed and the distant mewing of a gull.

Bobby came out and stood by my side, and I offered him a cigarette.

"Tank you!" he said.

He glanced up at the clearing sky, noted the change in the wind, felt the hint of coolness in the air.

"To-morrow, maybe," he decided, in Eskimo.

Meanwhile the music continued while cigarettes were smoked and little groups, chatting and laughing, broke up and re-formed. Then another dance, precisely like the first one—and then another—and another, till the dying glow of the sunset in the far north-western sky was replaced by the brighter gleaming of the sunrise in the far north-east, and the sub-Arctic dawn came again.

Chapter IV

WE LEAVE FOR THE BUTTON ISLANDS

THE motor-boat which was to take me to the Button Islands had been up on land all winter and her planks had dried. When she was put back in the water, in spite of the fact that she had been freshly painted and some of the more open seams had been recaulked, she leaked a little and I decided to put a load on board to force her down and soak her sides thoroughly so that they would swell up tight again.

Knowing the difficulty of obtaining petrol in the North, where each man orders for his own use only what he expects he will actually need during the summer and has none to spare, I had brought seventy gallons with me in ten-gallon drums. These we laid amidships on our bottom boards and the rest of the outfit—tools for digging, tents, food, sleeping bag, and so on—was disposed in such a way as to keep perishable things off the wet bottom of the boat.

We all worked at this, all except Lily that is, for she was temperamentally disinclined to any exertion which could be avoided. Bobby was standing in the motor-boat itself, receiving things as they were handed down by Mark who, in his turn, received them from Jenny. I was up in the warehouse, getting my stuff moved out of the carpenter's shop forward to the door, ready to be taken down the short wharf at the foot of which lay the boat.

Each time I came to the door with another box or

bundle, I could hear Mark and Jenny laughing. Of course, the Eskimos are generally cheerful and happy, and smiles are much more common than frowns, but I felt that such unusual and sustained mirth must have some special cause.

My soft *kamiks* made no sound as I carried a box, not just to the door, but right down to the foot of the wharf, so they didn't hear me coming. Mark, standing on a lower level than Jenny, for the tide was out, was just reaching up his hands for my rifle and shot-gun, each in a light canvas case.

"Tank you!" he said, most politely, in English as he took them.

"Tank you!" answered Jenny, equally deferentially, and then their laughter rang out again. Mark, this time, laughed even more loudly than did Jenny for, glancing up, he had caught sight of me over the end of the wharf.

In a flash, Jenny noted his upward glance, and saw me too. For a moment her face sobered. Would the white man be angry because they had mocked him and his language? After all, they hardly knew him at all.

Without a smile, I handed her the box I was carrying.

"Thank you!" I said.

Was there a smile in my eyes, or in my voice? Bobby and Mark had stopped to listen. Jenny listened, too, and stared earnestly at my face. Suddenly her expression changed; she had reached her decision.

"Tank you!" she said, as politely as possible, and all four of us burst into howls of laughter.

"*Taima!*" I announced, for the box I had brought down was the last one, and we had all had a smoke together, sitting just inside the warehouse door, out of the drizzle which was blowing from across the bay.

Bobby shook his head as he looked up at the sky, now

full of clouds. If this kept up, everything in the boat would get soaked through and through.

I scrambled down to the boat, opened up one of the bundles, and broke out two brand new tarpaulins, bright orange, stiff and strong-smelling, and we spread them out over the little mountain of gear in the boat, tucking the edges under the outermost cases. At last all was protected from the weather, and the boat as low in the water as we could force her.

"O.K.?" asked Bobby, using up twenty per cent. of his English in the one question.

"O.K." I agreed, and our first job together was done. Bobby, I could see, understood what was what and I had the man I wanted.

Now there was nothing to do but wait. Waiting is an art which one soon acquires perforce in the Arctic. I must wait while Bobby went to get his own stuff ready, and made arrangements for the care of his dogs, for he had decided to bring only two pups a few months old who could not look after themselves and a "white man's dog," Sammy, who was more of a pet than a working sled dog.

Then we must wait till the weather improved enough for us to run north along the west side of squarish Killinek Island, where we would lie in a native sealing camp, hidden in a deep and narrow strait, till conditions were just right for us to try a dash north to the Button Islands lying across Gray Straits, a stretch of water which even large steamers prefer to avoid unless it is fair weather.

Mark and Jenny started for their tent by way of the trail, while Bobby went round by sea in his kayak. He had been gone but a few moments and was not yet out of sight, when I heard a shot. I looked out to sea and saw Bobby paddling furiously. A moment or two later, he laid down his paddle and picked up his harpoon, which lay on the deck of his kayak ready to his reach. Poised with upright arm a moment, he suddenly threw it. Then he took up his paddle again and, holding it with one hand to steady his kayak, he hauled in on the harpoon line with the other. Fresh seal meat for Bobby and his family!

Later in the afternoon he came back to the Hudson's Bay Company's living quarters. The drizzle of the morning had become a steady downpour and, in spite of the tarpaulins, the stuff in the motor-boat might get wet from below, for the rain water would gradually fill the boat.

With a cheerful grin he suggested that we should unload everything again and once more put it in the warehouse where it would keep dry. It was the only reasonable thing to do and in an hour or so everything was where it had been. At least we were ahead of the game to the extent that the boat seemed to have taken up a good deal and would be dry as soon as we bailed the rain water out of her.

That evening, in the warm and comfortable kitchen, I was practising some string figures which I had learned during the spring. Primitive people in many parts of the world have larger or shorter repertoires of these intricate games and the Eskimo have a paticularly complex series. Our familiar "cat's cradle" is elementary indeed in comparison with many that are well known in the North. These games have been studied by anthropologists in the hope that their geographical distribution might furnish clues to the problems of racial migrations and culture diffusions.

Those I had learned were from the south-western parts of the United States, and simple indeed, but I had hoped that some of them would be unfamiliar to the Eskimos and of sufficient interest to get them started on their own patterns. I need hardly have worried about getting them interested for they were always willing to show me any number of them.

While I was practising my little tricks, I noticed Tola

watching me as she cleared things up. Soon she called Kitty's attention to what I was doing. Kitty was an Eskimo orphan girl of about eighteen employed, like Tola, by the Hudson's Bay Company as a house servant.

As soon as they had finished their work, they came to watch me. I showed them a simple Navaho figure called "The Door" which was new to them, but they were both complete masters of it after the first attempt. Then I showed them one or two others which they picked up just as readily.

Then they volunteered to show me some. At once I was completely lost. They appeared to delight in the very complexity of the figures they formed, and minutes seemed to go by as they wove their fingers dexterously in and out of the apparent tangles, even using their teeth as extra hands, and their feet too if the figure demanded it.

It was quite impossible for me to duplicate their figures, for I was bewildered after the first move or two. Later on, they condescended to my level and taught me two very simple tricks of the kind they do to amuse little children.

Next morning Bobby arrived with his sailboat and all his family and possessions loaded on it. All his possessions that is, with the exception of his winter stuff for which he could have no use during the summer.

With him was the one remaining member of the family whom I had not yet met—little Jimmy, or Shimmy, as they pronounce his name.

Jimmy was four; he was, without exception, the dirtiest and the happiest little urchin I have ever encountered. I was told in my childhood that the word "can't" is not to be found in the bright lexicon of youth; the word missing from little Jimmy's lexicon was "don't." Never had he been told not to do this, that, or the other and, as a completely natural result he did this, that and the other whenever the spirit moved him, and it moved him with a

" All the girls had changed to their best clothes "

Port Burwell. The H.B.C. store carries a flag. No. 1
Warehouse is opposite, on the right

continuous motion. Never for a moment was he still, except when he was asleep; never was he annoying, never anything but a delightful and adorable child—well, almost never.

At first he was shy in the presence of the *kablunah*, as was natural enough for, though he had seen a good many white men, principally in the service of the Hudson's Bay Company and the Mounted Police, I was a stranger and an unknown quantity. I grinned at him once or twice after shaking hands all round and then took no further notice of him for a day or two, by which time he grew used to having me about.

There was one sad thing about little Jimmy, and that was the state of his teeth. The Eskimos, as a people, have amazingly fine teeth and in the skulls of Eskimos long dead one will see that this has been their good fortune for many years back into the past. But not so to-day, for wherever they have access to our foodstuffs, including flour, sugar, lard, and soft boiled foods, their teeth deteriorate. Bobby had fine teeth, clean and healthy; apparently he had not had many opportunities to get white man's food during his childhood, but little Jimmy's teeth were rank with caries and he will probably have bad teeth all his life as a result of improper diet during his childhood.

Once more we loaded my stuff into the motor-boat which, now that it had had a good soaking, was a good deal nearer to being watertight. The weather was still wet and foggy, but there was no foretelling when it might clear and, as it was better to be right on hand, waiting on the shore of Gray Straits ready to take advantage of a break in the weather, we decided to waste no further time but to start out immediately.

The only dissenter to this proposal was the motor. It simply refused to start. Davidee, the Eskimo attached to

D

the Post in a more or less official capacity as boat tender and engineer, coaxed it in every way his experience suggested, but the cold, dispirited hunk of metal sat glumly in sullen dignity, permitting every imaginable familiarity but offering no response.

Suddenly, catching Davidee by surprise, it gave vent to a startling series of explosions and released a cloud of foul blue smoke. Davidee backed out of range, pleased and smiling.

"*Taima!*" he announced, and Bobby laid hold of the slack in the tow-rope fastened to his sailboat, ready to take up the strain and ease her into motion.

At last we were on our way.

Sitting in the after end of the motor-boat, puffing on a cigarette and saying nothing, was Mark. His eyes were fixed on a little group of tents by the stream which runs into the north side of the harbour. Among them was Emily's tent, and she would certainly hear the motor. She might come out to watch him leave.

Mark's eyes followed the tents as they receded into the distance. One tent in particular.

In a minute or two our bows would turn south. Then she came. She didn't wave, for that is not an Eskimo custom, but she did stand and watch us, and it was clear that she knew Mark was on board with us. She might not see him again for several weeks.

She stood in the sloping entrance of her tent, her head and shoulders covered with a brilliant red shawl, and the rest of her still inside, as these people do, with the shortest one standing in front and the tallest behind, all in a row, head above head, so that everybody can see, the edges of the cloth clutched in a crescendo of hands.

Mark stood up so that there should be no doubt that he had seen her, and then reseated himself. He looked forward and his expression seemed a trifle anxious as he saw that Davidee, too, had been watching Emily. Davidee was not going to be away for more than a couple of days, and he wasn't the kind of fellow to waste a good opportunity.

Too bad, but there was nothing that Mark could do about it. Davidee spun the wheel, the rudder swung over, and we turned south.

Near the old Moravian Mission there is a short cut from the harbour to the open sea, a short cut which can be used only at high tide, for at any other time it was impassable even for a rowboat.

Just then the tide was low, so the route through the Mission trickle was not feasible and we had to go all the way round the island which forms the west side of the harbour. Not much farther after all, only two or three miles perhaps, not enough to worry about.

By now the motor was warm and comfortable and she chugged along with a steady, serious-minded rhythm which was encouraging and gave one a sense of confidence in her ability to get us to our destination. Davidee stayed near by, with the steering-wheel under his hand. Bobby stood erect in the bow with a keen eye out for drifting ice and pieces of floating wood.

Lily and little Jimmy were snuggled down as low as they could get amidships on their own boat, keeping as warm as possible, while Jenny sat back aft with the tiller in her hand. She didn't seem to mind the cold, wet fog which enveloped us, and the boats, and the whole of our surroundings, as long as she had a cigarette to puff on. The hood of her *attigi* was up over her head, but that was her only admission that the weather was not all that it might have been.

All about us was a thick fog. For any larger craft, progress would have been impossible, but we chugged along so slowly that there was no danger of our hitting anything.

We could coast along within a hundred yards of the shore,
for we could see land on our starboard side all the way,
and so we made our way from point to point through the
fog, never astray and never in the least doubt as to our
position. Five knots was our speed and we had been running a little over an hour, so we were well round the
bottom of the island, and running north.

Everything I touched was wet with the fog which had
settled in beaded droplets on the thwarts, the gunwales, the
equipment, on my clothes, on the clothing of everybody
else. Our limit of visibility was a hundred yards or less
and things seemed to appear quite suddenly ahead of us;
floating pieces of blue-green ice, some large, some small,
many of them worn and thawed into fantastic shapes by
their long immersion in water just a little warmer than
their chilly selves, blown on by winds a couple of degrees
above the freezing point; occasional logs of driftwood,
some of them large enough for two or three seagulls to
stand on while the currents and the tide carried them, free
of charge, as they scanned the passing surface of the sea
for anything edible.

Now and then a piece of driftwood was judged large
enough to be worth going a little out of our direct course
for, and it would be scooped up and thrown into Bobby's
boat. In time it would be dry enough to use for fuel, or
it might prove suitable for making some such thing as a
harpoon shaft or a sled runner. The seagulls, deprived of
their raft, flew off with sullen, slow-flapping wings, utter-
ing hoarse cries of disapproval.

A chill, wet wind started blowing and the fog gave up
all efforts at further resistance and turned to rain, cold,
penetrating, with no intention of stopping for hours to
come.

"*Ikki?*" asked Bobby.

I grinned politely, and lied.

"No, not cold. All right."

Bobby turned to David, or Davidee, as he called him, for nearly all the English names adopted by the Eskimos of the eastern Arctic have been looted from the Bible by the missionaries and then have had an " e " tacked on the end by the natives themselves, so we have Davidee, and Jonassee, and Marcussee, and many others.

Bobby turned to Davidee and said something, gesturing towards the starboard side where the land lay. Suddenly we turned sharply to the right, as though we were about to run straight into the sheer cliff ahead of us. Another sudden turn brought us into the mouth of an almost invisible cleft which led to a snug little cove with high cliffs all round it.

It was hardly a quarter of a mile across in any direction, and surely no breath of wind could ever blow in here. The tide rose and fell in it, as could be seen by the water-washed sides, and bits of ice drifted in and out, scouring the rocks, but it was just the kind of place which a pirate or a smuggler might spend a lifetime wishing for without ever finding it.

Here we found two other boats sheltering from the rough weather. One of them, a motor-boat, I recognized as belonging to an Eskimo for I had seen her in harbour at Port Burwell the day before. The other was a sailboat, something like Bobby's but perhaps a little larger. For some reason which I never fathomed, she was named *The Tiger*.

We pulled in alongside her and Bobby jumped aboard with a line which he made fast. His sailboat came alongside us, and Jenny made her fast too. The sudden silence when the motor stopped, the cessation of movement, the pit-like surroundings which would have filled Doré with an itch for his brushes, and the steady relentless downpour of the rain, all combined to produce a most curious and

impressive effect. Then I realized that what I had mis-
taken for silence was in reality a continuous, steady,
unvarying noise, the roaring hiss of the rain falling into
the grey-green water. It was like a prolonged sound of
escaping steam.

Davidee stood up and stretched, so did Bobby and Mark.
Jenny shook back the hood of her *attigi* and brushed her
damp hair away from her forehead.

"Tea?" asked Bobby.

I nodded and smiled. Tea sounded like a good idea.
Never could a mug-up be more welcome. I clambered
aboard *The Tiger*, and, following Bobby's example,
lowered myself over the edge of the four-foot-square hatch-
way into her diminutive hold.

Here a mug-up was in full swing. There must have been
twenty Eskimos clustered round the extemporized stove
on which stood the tea kettle. They were all dressed in
more or less shabby variations of the costume that my own
family was wearing; they were all wet from the rain and
steaming nicely now that they were in a warm, dry place
and out of the wet.

There was a rich, rank smell.

An aged woman who was, I presume, the wife of the
owner of *The Tiger* and therefore my hostess, reached
back into the gloomy spaces behind her and pulled forward a folded caribou skin. She placed this beside her
and, with a hospitable grin, motioned to me to sit down.

Then she fumbled in a grub box at her elbow and produced an enamel mug. It was not a new mug; in fact, it
was considerably battered. All the good mugs were
already in use, and she had no other left. She dipped it
into the steaming kettle of tea, wiped off the drip with a
grimy finger, licked it off, and handed me the mug.

Her smile was friendly, cordial. To refuse, even to hesi-
tate would have been unkind, an unpardonable affront.

But her mug, or rather, *my* mug, was revoltingly dirty, or, at any rate, I felt it must be and caribou hairs floated on top of the tea.

Suddenly, my problem was solved. My hostess was at my left. What more natural than to take the mug with my left hand?

I did so and noted with some satisfaction that the enamel was a little less chipped on that side. Under pretext of removing a large tea-leaf, I managed to wipe my finger along the edge where I was soon to place my lips. It was rough and raw.

I drank. The tea was hot and strong and very welcome. Why had I made such a fuss about it? It did smell of seal-oil, but I can't honestly say that it tasted of it too. There was plenty of sugar in it, though no milk, and I downed it gladly, straining out the caribou hairs and most of the tea-leaves with my clenched teeth as I did so.

Then I passed the mug back for a refill.

"*Peeouyuk?*" she asked.

"*Ee. Peeouyuk.*" I answered. "Yes. Good."

Back came my mug, filled to the brim again, and with it a large hunk of fresh bannock.

Now that all the forms of politeness had been fulfilled, my hostess and her friends were free to turn to Bobby with questions about his protégé.

They all knew who I was, where we were going, what we expected to do there, and all about that. But why? Why?

Why on earth did a white man want to come all these miles, just to poke about the places where the old people had lived?

Bobby didn't know. Davidee didn't know. Jenny had no answer. Poor Lily wasn't even asked.

I was the only one there who did know—and I couldn't tell them.

Because of my inability to talk with my hosts, I was left out of most of the conversation and so had ample opportunity to look about me and see what was to be seen. Evidently *The Tiger's* owner was going off for a season of sealing. Rolled up in the hold I could see his tent, his bedding, and sundry boxes presumably containing tools, clothes, and the few simple cooking utensils they use. Close at hand was the dismembered carcass of a seal from which several pieces of meat and blubber had already been cut. It smelt of raw meat but it was not unpleasant. The liver had already disappeared and the entrails, in all probability, thrown to the dogs.

These were huddled in a disconsolate group at the aft end of the hold, where they could not get at the seal meat. They were lying in a tangled mass of noses, paws, and tails, trying to get dry and warm, for they had all got soaking wet in the rain. Eskimo dogs detest boats, for they get seasick and will run off into the hills, often enough, if they suspect they are going to be caught and put on board.

In the centre of the circle of Eskimos was the stove. No old-fashioned soapstone lamp this, but an improvised metal affair made from a forty-five gallon oil-drum. The drums are cylindrical in shape and, to make a stove, a section a little over a foot long is cut off one end with a hammer and cold chisel. It is a long job, and by no means a silent one. Occasionally the other end is cut off too, just a couple of inches deep, but this is an unnecessary refinement and comparatively rare; moreover, it prevents making another stove from the other end of the drum.

Three holes are cut in the stove; one at the bottom to admit a draught; a larger one on the top, to put a kettle or a frying-pan on, and for stoking up; and a smaller one, also in the top, for the stove pipe.

On board *The Tiger* the stove stood in a large wooden tray filled with sand. This served to keep the fire from the bottom boards of the boat and also to make the stove air-tight, by heaping the sand up round the sides.

The draught is regulated by a little pile of flat stones in front of the air intake. This can be built up higher or lowered, admitting more or less air, and so controlling the draught. The outlet pipe, an ordinary four-inch stove-pipe, has no damper in it. In some cases there is a sheet of thin metal to cover the burner hole or a thin flat stone may be used if there is no kettle on the stove.

Driftwood is the usual fuel in these stoves, and often a strip of dripping blubber is added to make a quick, hot fire. Greasy bones, too, burn well. Sometimes a few bits of coal are added, for there is a place in the harbour at Port Burwell where coal may be picked up from the tide flats at very low water, where it was dropped from a steamship which once went aground there. This unusual source of supply is now near exhaustion.

After a quarter of an hour or so everybody had finished drinking tea, and we all were comparatively warm and dry again.

" *Taima?* " asked Bobby, getting to his feet as he caught my nodded assent.

Outside, on deck again, we found that the rain had stopped and it even looked as if the fog might have lifted outside our little cove. Once more we took our places in the motor-boat, cast off from *The Tiger* and turned bows towards the entrance. This time the motor started with no hesitation, being still warm.

Again we turned to the north. The fog had indeed cleared considerably and we could see much farther ahead than had been possible before. Far beyond our sight the coast line stretched and curved and, on our port side, off-shore islands were dotted here and there.

On many of the headlands and hill-tops stood a cairn, a pile of stones built into a slender, tapering pillar about

six feet high. These have been built, in most cases, by
the Eskimos, though some of them are to be attributed
to surveyors charting the coast line and mapping the
land.

Inuksuk is the Eskimo name for a cairn, derived from
inuk, a man, and meaning "that which looks like a man."
The name is a good one, for often enough the cairn does
look much like a man standing on the high point, and
gazing steadfastly out to sea. Their principal purpose
is to serve as landmarks and an Eskimo knows the shape
and colour of every one in his district. Should he be
overtaken by fog or bad weather he will often be able to
save himself from going astray by the timely sight of a
familiar cairn.

After half a dozen more miles we swung to starboard
through a narrow channel. This brought us to the north
side of Killinek Island, with the east end of Hudson Straits
on our port side. Continuing to coast along, we slipped
past a little promontory on which sat an Eskimo with
a rifle, waiting for a chance for a shot at a seal. Behind
him was a flattish area of a little more than an acre and a
sheltered little bay. Here we came to rest.

Bobby hauled out the smaller of my two tents and
handed it up to Jenny, who had climbed ashore from the
sailboat after making fast. She carried the tent up the
steep, rocky beach to the flat and awaited my arrival
before deciding just where it should be pitched. I
selected a spot near the steep 'cliffs which rose a hundred
feet inland, for here it would be sheltered from at least
one direction.

In a few minutes the tent was up and my sleeping
bag was in it, as well as a grub box with a few odds and
ends of white man's food supplies. There was no knowing how long or how short our stay here might be, but
it was certainly not worth while unloading all my stuff,

only to reload it all a day or so later. We had done quite enough of that as it was.

Hardly was the tent pitched when *The Tiger* appeared round the point and tied up in the same little bay that we lay in. Her people came ashore with their tents and all their belongings and made camp. This suited Bobby admirably, for he and Mark and Lily and Jenny and little Jimmy were all able to move in with *The Tiger* people and he didn't have to bother putting up his own tent. Crowded? Yes, but what of that? They were all the warmer and it was nice to have a lot of people to talk to. In another tent, Davidee found congenial lodgings.

Soon another family arrived and, before long, there were five more tents in addition to my own. There had been but one when we first came. A little village had suddenly materialized. Here they might stay for a few days or, if the sealing were not up to expectations, they might all move off again at an hour's notice, leaving hardly a trace of their ever having been there.

Chapter V

AN ESKIMO SEALING CAMP

IN summer the east end of Hudson Straits is, perhaps, one of the foggiest places in the eastern Arctic. As many as twenty-six foggy days have been counted in the month of July, and the average is fourteen. Warm winds blowing from the land, now bare of snow and exposed to the rays of the sun, play upon the cold waters flowing from the wide expanse of Hudson Bay and Foxe Basin and fog is the result.

On the morning after our arrival at the sealing camp, the fog was just as thick as it had been the day before and it didn't look as though we should have any luck as far as getting across Gray Straits to the Button Islands was concerned.

Bobby came out of his friends' tent and looked about him. His eyes were directed principally upwards for we were so fenced about by hills and cliffs that one couldn't see very far in any other direction. Above us ragged streamers of mist and cloud scraped across the rocky hill-tops, combed to shreds on the jagged pinnacles by the wind which, while blasting huge masses of fog away, continuously formed more by blowing comparatively warm air over cold water.

"*Taktok!*" Bobby exclaimed, and shook his head. "Fog!"

There would be no crossing that day.

The only thing to do while waiting was to explore my

surroundings, so I struck off inland for a walk. About two hundred yards from the tents I found a group of five ruined Eskimo igloos, not very old, but still well worthy of examination.

An igloo is a house, but not necessarily one built of blocks of snow; it is any kind of a house, as distinguished from a *tupik*, which is a tent. The snow house is not nearly as common a feature of Eskimo life as most people seem to believe, in fact, there are many Eskimos who have never seen one. Common enough, usual indeed, in the central Arctic, they are rare, if not quite unknown, in Alaska and as far east as the delta of the huge Mackenzie River. In Greenland, too, they are seldom used; even on the coast of the Labrador they are now built less frequently than they used to be.

These five igloos on which I had stumbled had been built of large stones, many of them as much as a man could readily lift, and slabs of turf; an occasional large bone from the carcass of a whale gleamed white in the side of the wall.

The roofs, made of logs of driftwood covered with sods, had fallen in and not much was left of the igloos but circular depressions with walls some two or three feet high. The entrance to each house was a narrow passage, a few feet long, facing on to the sea. As these igloos were not very old, these entrance tunnels were still quite easily distinguished.

Round about the walls the grass was lush and green, a sure sign that the igloos were of comparatively recent date. There is always a good deal of waste animal matter, garbage in fact, thrown out near an Eskimo dwelling. The dogs devour most of it, but there is enough to enrich the soil and a plentiful crop of vegetation appears, the luxuriance of the grass affording convincing evidence of the fertility of the soil. In the course of time, the supply of animal matter becomes exhausted and the crop grows less; the lushness diminishes until, after the lapse of who knows how many years, there is no visible distinction in the vegetation at all and the former presence of an igloo may be very difficult to detect.

These igloos, at any rate, were visible enough. No one could possibly overlook them, even if one took no interest at all in matters archæological. Signs of European contact, such as pieces of glazed pottery and bits of ironware, neither of which was known to the Eskimos in their primitive condition, were scattered about. Nevertheless, these houses stood some fifty feet above sea level and far from the water, for it must have been three or four hundred yards down the pleasant little valley in which they were clustered, to the beach. Access to the sea could be gained also by the way I had taken, but this was over a high rocky ridge across which it would have been very awkward to carry a kayak or drag a seal. The land must have risen some thirty feet since they were first built if they stood originally near sea level, and most Eskimo dwellings to-day are found as close to the water's edge as is reasonably possible.

Jenny joined me after half an hour or so, and we poked about together, looking for anything of interest which might turn up. There was not much to be found in the old igloos themselves as far as we could see, for the lush green grass covered everything and it would have been necessary to do some digging in order to bring to light any specimens that might lie under the sod. This would involve unloading and uncrating tools and other equipment, which I had already decided not to do at this place.

Almost invisible among the rocks which littered the near-by hillsides were a number of Eskimo graves, heaps of large stones so disposed as to form a sort of box. One side might be a single large rock left in its original position and, parallel with it a couple of feet away, a row of other stones would be so placed as to form a wall five or six feet long and two feet high. The two ends are also closed and large flat stones are laid across in such a way as to form a lid. In some of these graves all the cracks and crevices between the large stones were carefully filled; in others, not nearly so much care had been taken in the construction of the grave, and one wondered what reasons lay behind these differences. Was it a matter of lack of time, or were the graves which showed so little care built in the winter when stones were not so easily seen beneath the snow or were difficult to pry from their frozen beds? Or was it a lack of affection, the burial of a comparative stranger perhaps?

Peering down through the open crevices in some of the graves we could see the skull and the long bones of the skeleton as it lay at full length on its back. In other cases, there was nothing to be seen. We lifted the lids off some of the more accessible ones to see if any objects had been placed in the grave with the body as was sometimes done, but drew blank in any of those we opened. Jenny helped me to replace the covering slabs, but it was clear that she thought that this consideration for the departed was quite needless. Neither she nor anybody else knew who these people were, and they had no objection at all to my examining the graves.

Many of the burials were evidently fairly old, for the rocks which formed the cysts were covered with black lichens and these take many years to grow in the sub-Arctic. A rock will show, by the absence of lichens, on one or more surfaces, if it has been moved comparatively recently, though that may mean anything from fifty to a hundred years ago.

Knowing that objects were sometimes hidden close

to a grave rather than actually in it, I started searching among the rocks near by and it was not long before I found a little cache, almost like a miniature grave itself, and in it were two lumps of iron pyrites, which the old people used as a means of striking fire by hitting them together and making sparks; these they caught on a little pad of dry tinder and, by gentle blowing, fanned into a glowing mass hot enough to start a fire. With the iron pyrites was an awl, made of bone, and a skin scraper chipped from stone. This, then, was the grave of a woman, for it was customary to provide the dead with the things they have used in this world and which they are apt to need during their journeyings in the world to come.

Another grave cache yielded part of a stone knife, a bone knife handle, a miniature harpoon head, and the inflator and plug for a sealskin float used in summer seal hunting. This was a man's grave and he had been given the things he needed to secure his food while he wandered in the land of the spirits.

Jenny had evidently found something, too, for she called excitedly, *"Kablunah!"* I don't think she ever knew my name, nor did Bobby for that matter, and now that she wanted to attract my attention, she hardly knew what name to use. *Kablunah* means eyebrows, or the one having eyebrows, and is the usual Eskimo name for a white man. These people have surprisingly little hair on their faces, or anywhere else on their bodies for that matter, except on their heads where it is long, straight, thick and of a shining, glossy black. Evidently the heavy eyebrows that some white men have attracted attention and the name has stuck.

Jenny grinned a little apologetically when I reached her and pointed to a larger cache, apparently not connected with a grave at all. Here the finds were a good

The start of a kayak race

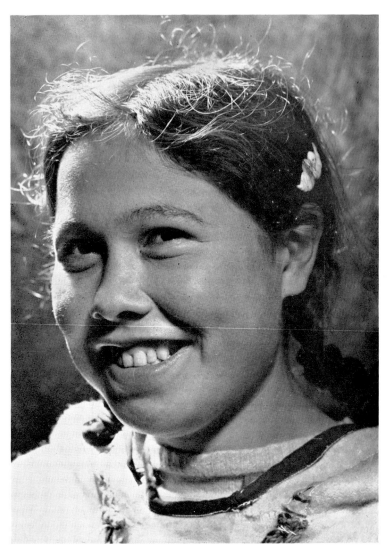

" The Eskimos have amazingly fine teeth "

deal more interesting. First in importance were two wooden bows, each made of a single stave of driftwood. They were rather sadly warped out of their original shape by being forced into a crevice in the rocks and had held this unnatural position for years. There were also two whetstones, a small skin scraper, two canine teeth of a polar bear, harpoon heads and arrow heads, a drinking tube made from the hollow bone of a large bird's wing, a small buckle of walrus ivory, and various odds and ends which might well have come from a man's tool bag. The bows were especially interesting, for but few specimens of the weapons used by these Killinek people before they had access to firearms have found their way into museums.

While we were discussing our finds, the rain began again and we moved back to the shelter of the tents. One of the men had just killed a seal and, after the women had cut it up, he gathered up the intestines and offal to feed his dogs. These dog feedings are a sight to be seen and remembered.

While the seal is being butchered, the dogs, well knowing what is in store for them, sit round in a ravenous circle watching the women at work on the carcass, but not venturing too close for they know they would be driven off with stones. At last the work is done and the dogs, wise in the ways of mankind, rise to their feet. Then one of the men (not a woman as a rule, for the dogs are frantic in their eagerness and might do her harm) carries the offal a little way and throws it down in a more or less open space.

The dogs and their food seem to reach the spot simultaneously. Each dog seizes the nearest mouthful and tries to make off with it but, as all the organs are still attached to each other, the resulting tangle and confusion is amazing.

E

What snarling and snapping, what deep-throated growls and ominous threats, what hurried and apologetic droppings of desirable portions if a small dog has taken what a big dog demands! Round and round they twist and writhe till each dog is enmeshed in coils of sinuous intestines and each white coat is barred with blood-red stripes and splotches which will remain till time and the rain remove these traces of their grisly version of the Maypole dance.

There's one thing about the North that no visitor will ever forget—the howling of the dogs in chorus. It doesn't take very much to start them, often enough the ship's siren will do the trick. One dog will begin by putting back his head, his nose turned to the skies, and emitting a long and doleful wail. All the dogs within hearing, and there may be as many as a couple of hundred of them at ship time, full of canine sympathy and compassion, will join with him in his lament, and soon every dog in the camp will be singing in the choir.

It is anything but unpleasant; indeed, it has a spine-tingling, awe-inspiring quality which makes a strong and indelible impression on those who hear it. Old-timers sometimes curse the howling and threaten the dogs with stones, but not one of them, now exiled to southern lands, ever hears a dog howl without remembering the husky chorus and wondering wistfully if he will ever hear it again.

Seals are, of course, the important thing in the economy of the coast-dwelling Eskimo. Not only are they the most important single item in the food supply, with caribou second, but seal leather is used for boots and lines and floats, occasionally even now for summer tents, clumsy and heavy though they be. The oil provides fuel for the winter lamps, and the raw blubber is often burnt in the stoves.

The seals of the Atlantic side of the Arctic are not the fur seal, from which fur coats for the ladies are made, but hair seals. The fur seals are confined to the Pacific Ocean. The fur of the hair-seal pup, or whitecoat, is fluffy, short, and it makes excellent lining for children's clothing and for bedroom slippers. Once this white coat is lost, the hair seal has nothing much to offer in the way of fur.

The watch for seals is constant and unremitting. The little flat on which we were camped terminated in an out-jutting rocky point on which was a rudely constructed wind-break built of slabs of rock. In the shelter of this sat a seal-hunter; almost all day somebody would be sitting there, armed with a ·30-30 rifle. Immediately at hand was his kayak, ready to launch without delay.

Shooting seals requires a quick eye, which the Eskimo has, and a sure aim, which he usually has not, for when a seal comes up to breathe only his head appears and, if there is the least suggestion of danger, any movement even, down he goes in a flash. His large and prominent eyes are so set that a wide angle can be inspected without turning the head.

Continuous vigilance is demanded of the hunter. He may not doze as he sits waiting, for seals may appear at any moment, at any distance, in any direction, so long as it be in water. There may be but one seal, or there may be a school of ten; they may stay two seconds, just long enough for one quick expulsion of stale air and one quick inward breath, or they may stay nearly a minute; they may keep fairly still, or they may toss about, playing in the water, bobbing up and down like girls at a bathing beach; so it is always a matter of a quick eye and a sure aim.

Even then, hitting the seal is not all that is needed.

The hunter must get to the dead or wounded animal as soon as he can or, even now, he may lose it. If it is but slightly wounded, it may escape by its own efforts. If killed stone dead as, being shot in the head, it may well be, it can sink and disappear entirely. The specific gravity of a seal's body is almost exactly that of the salt water in which it lives. This is an advantage to the seal since it reduces the effort necessary to enable it to rise or sink in the water in its pursuit of its food. In summer, the seal loses some of its fat, the specific weight increases, making it heavier than salt water, and so a dead seal will often sink before the hunter can secure it with a thrust of his harpoon.

Sometimes a seal lost in this way will form gas enough to bring it to the surface again in even so short a time as half an hour, but this is the exception rather than the rule.

That evening I discovered that Jenny was getting a little worried about my meals, for which she evidently felt herself responsible. I had managed to find a handful of potatoes, some sweet biscuits, and a couple of oranges in my supplies, but this was poor fare for one leading an active life scrambling over rocky landscapes in cold and windy weather, and often pretty wet into the bargain.

She called me over to where the carcass of a freshly killed seal was lying just inside the tent, at the right as one entered. It was not a very attractive object, a somewhat disorganized mass of meat, bones, blood and blubber.

Blubber, which most schoolchildren believe the Eskimo eats as we do toffee, is the layer of fat which lies under the skin of the seal and other Arctic mammals and acts as insulating material, making possible life in water continuously but little above the freezing point of salt water, about 29° Fahrenheit.

Bits of this blubber had been cut off as occasion required for fuel, and part of the meat was in the pot, stewing slowly on top of the stove. The meat is dark in colour and unappetizing in appearance.

Jenny turned back the skin and showed me the liver lying under a fold of it.

"*Peeouyuk?*" she asked, meaning, as far as I could gather, "Does this look good to you?"

"*Ee!*" I agreed, and she smiled with relief. In a few minutes she had sliced up some boiled potatoes left from a previous meal and they were sizzling in the pan with a thin slice of the fresh liver.

It was most excellent stuff to eat. It may be a trifle more full-flavoured than calf's liver, but when fresh it is a dish at which no man need turn up his nose.

Jenny watched me stow away the whole batch and was eager to fry some more. However, I remembered the effect liver had on the family cat at home, and refrained. Then hot tea, and some of the sweet biscuits, which we shared, and I was ready for more local explorations on the morrow.

Our second day at the sealing camp was still wet and windy and my unheated tent was unpleasantly damp and cold. I slept well, for my sleeping bag was warm enough, even though I had little beneath it but the mossy soil; but once I crawled out of my bag into the outer atmosphere it was definitely chilly, even though the calendar proclaimed it was the second of August.

An elderly Eskimo was waiting to see me after breakfast. He made me understand what it was he wanted to discuss with me by slipping off his parka and his shirt to show me a red and swollen arm. He explained, in pantomime, that he had cut his hand slightly and that the wound had become infected. Now the pain was all up his arm and even down his side into his breast. A few angry-looking spots in his arm-pit were, he felt, part of the same complex of symptoms. What was he to do for it?

An Eskimo takes it for granted that a white man is a doctor, but I was quite unequal to explaining hot fomentations and a poultice in Eskimo and there were no sulpha drugs to fall back upon. It must have been a puzzled Eskimo to whom I suggested what simple remedies I could and advised to go back to Port Burwell to await the return of the *Nascopie* with a real doctor on board. However, he was grateful for my efforts and smiled with pleasure and good cheer.

"*Nago!*" he said. "*Nago!*"

"*Nago?*" I repeated, with a note of enquiry.

"Tank you!" he translated, and laughed aloud. We parted on the best of good terms, but I felt that I had not been able to do much for my first patient. I was to have a number of others, before I got back.

No sooner had he gone than two women, older than most of the others in camp, came over to where I was sitting. One of them had a small, grey soapstone pot, a model of the kind that used to be used for cooking in. It was a rectangular affair, about the size of an ordinary brick or perhaps a little smaller and the walls were about a quarter of an inch thick. The sides were gracefully curved; it was a very fine specimen.

In the bottom, a hole had been drilled, a common way of "killing" a pot before laying it on or near a grave. Some say this is done so that the "spirit" of the pot may be free to travel in the land of the shades with the spirit of its owner, but I am unable to say whether this is what the Eskimos themselves think about it.

I understood the women to say that they had found this pot on a grave not very far away and, knowing my interest in such things, they had brought it to me. I was very much pleased with their gift and gave vent, quite unconsciously, to a long *"Eeeee!"* of delight and admiration. This reaction to their little present was so typically Eskimo rather than white that they were both much amused, but it was quite a surprise to me for I had never so expressed myself in my life before, and it was not until I had done so that I realized that it was just what they themselves would have said in similar circumstances. I gave them a package of cigarettes in return for the little pot, and everybody was well pleased with the transaction.

I noticed that one of these two women was tattooed, as were some whom I had seen at Port Burwell. The custom is, or rather was, widespread in the Arctic and, though the pattern varies somewhat in different parts of the North, the main elements of the design are fairly standardized. A typical design, which I had seen the year before at Cape Wolstenholme at the western end of Hudson Strait, consisted of seven double parallel lines running down the chin and a "lazy Y" on each cheek.

In a few cases the design may be pricked in, but the more usual method is to sew the marks in. A needle, steel in these days but originally of bone or ivory, is threaded with sinew or cotton which has been loaded with a mixture of grease and lampblack, taken from the bottom of the cooking pot. A pinch of skin is taken up in the left fingers and the needle is stitched through. As the sinew is drawn through the two perforations it leaves some of its load of lampblack under the skin and an indelible mark remains. Actually the pigment is a dense and pure black but, when seen through a thin layer of slightly yellowish skin, a blue-black tinge results.

Tattooing is dying out with the older generation of women; though I have seen many older women who bore the marks, I have seen few if any young ones with any. In the old days, not only faces, but wrists, arms, and even breasts were tattooed among the women; the men, as a rule, had none. It is said that the operation, which was performed about the time of puberty, was not a pleasant one!

Still the fog blew across the hill-tops and filled the valleys. Bobby and Davidee came to ask my permission to take the motor-boat (for she had my petrol in her tanks) and go after seals, as they could cover more ground in that way and, too, had a better chance of securing a wounded seal before it sank. They were away most of the afternoon and returned with no less than four seals. Skinning and cleaning operations were soon under way on a big scale and all the women hard at work, a circle of ever-hungry, patient dogs watching every movement. For once, they got almost as much as they could eat.

Whenever I felt too cold for comfort I would go into one of the Eskimo tents to get warm. I was always made welcome, even though I could do no more than smile affably and grumble the word " *Taktok!* " trying to curse the fog by my very intonation, as I had heard Bobby do. They would smile in return and repeat " *Taktok* " to show that they understood my meaning and shared my disgust.

Even so the tents were not as comfortable as they might have been, for the rain, steadily falling, had loaded the vegetation on the hillsides to saturation and now the water was streaming down the slopes.

This is a land of very rapid run-off. If the weather has been fine for a few days, the land surface will have had a chance to dry; but as soon as rain falls the sphag-

num moss, lichens, and other plants begin to soak it
up. Soon they have absorbed all they can hold and then
the water spills over. First it trickles more or less aim-
lessly over the bare rock surfaces, then it gathers in little
puddles and pools, a little later it forms brooks and chattering rills. Soon these are cascading down in hundreds
along every slope, uniting in the valleys to make toler-
ably large streams and, on wide stretches of land, actual
rivers.

This is what happened now. All the hillside behind
us poured water down its flanks and the tents, nestling at
the foot of the slope, sometimes bridged sections of the
run-off. The Eskimos were all quite unperturbed. If
a little torrent ran right through their tent, they made no
effort to move to another site. Instead, they would
channel out a convenient bed for the nascent brook, lead
it away from the bedding, help it to steer clear of both the
seal-meat and the stove, and lead it out to one side just
before it flooded the entrance.

It was the children who most enjoyed these peewee
engineering works, which were left largely in their hands.
I came into a tent once and found Jenny and little Jimmy
hard at work building a miniature canal and taking it
quite as a matter of course, just as we think nothing of
sweeping up the autumn leaves on the lawn.

My little silk tent was wet too, but at least there were
no streams running through it. It was a new one that
season and looked startlingly clean, for it had hitherto
reposed safely in a canvas bag which kept it immaculate.
However, this unnatural purity was not to last long. Our
neighbours had landed but a few minutes after we did,
and my nice new tent immediately attracted the curious
attention of one of their dogs.

He sniffed round it with growing excitement, until he
was able to announce to his team-mates and acquaintances

that he had found a *new* tent, sniff, sniff, absolutely new, sniff, sniff, that had never yet been initiated, sniff, sniff, and, by golly, he was going to be the first. He was, but by no means the last. Singly and in ceremonious little groups, with much stiff-legged walking and strutting, every husky dog in that sealing camp added his autograph. My tent was no longer new, or clean.

Chapter VI

CROSSING PERILOUS GRAY STRAITS

BRIGHT sunlight slashing across my tent gave me the first news that there had been a change in the weather.

As I dressed, I felt a difference in everything. Not only was the sun shining strongly when I poked my head out of the door, but the wind had dropped to a light breeze and it was obviously going to be a warm day. Small icebergs, glittering white with translucent, deep-blue shadows, drifted rapidly past, borne along by the rushing tide while seagulls swooped and cried overhead.

I heard the clatter of a boat-hook thrown on deck and, turning, saw that *The Tiger's* people were getting their stuff aboard; they, too, had had enough of the dreary fogs and mists of the last few days and they all laughed and chattered happily as they worked.

Moving day holds no terrors for an Eskimo family. Anything done so often must be reduced to its simplest terms. Therefore everything is portable and is carried on board in armfuls and bundles. All hands work at it, father, mother, and children, each carrying whatever he can manage. There are rolls of bedding, consisting of blankets procured from the Hudson's Bay Company store as well as caribou skins, pretty badly worn often enough. Then there are the mattresses, thin mats of willow twigs, pencil thick, lashed together side by side and heads to tails with cords of braided sinew. These serve to keep the

bedding off the snow in winter so that it won't get
frozen down and, in summer, to keep it drier than it
would otherwise be, when beds have to be made on damp
ground.

To-day wooden boxes take the place of the native sealskin bags in which the women carry their spare clothes,
their sewing kits, and whatever other possessions they
may have; boxes, or bags, are used by the men to carry
their tools and repair kits. Then there are rolls of seal
hides for making boots and other necessary articles; there
are, likely enough, slabs of fresh seal-meat which have
to be taken along too. Convenient hand-holds are cut in
these, for they would be awkward to pick up otherwise;
as it is they are often so heavy and slippery that it takes
two women to handle one of them.

Last of all, except for the tent itself, comes the stove.
The pipe will already have been taken off and laid on
the near-by rocks to cool, and the stove itself turned upside
down and rolled out of the tent for the same purpose.

Then the stones are rolled away from the tent wall,
the ropes are slacked off and down comes the tent. The
slacking of the first rope is a signal every dog in sight
has been waiting for; once a rope is slacked off, the tent
becomes, in dog law, no longer a man's tent but the public
domain, and he who wills may enter, though it was
strictly forbidden but a minute before.

Simultaneously they dash forward to the spot where
the seal-meat was kept, generally on a little bench of
loosely laid stones, to grab for what trifles may have
slipped down unnoticed and to lick at the pools of con-
gealed blood that have dripped from the bleeding carcasses.

It's always the maddest kind of mêlée, with the big
dogs trying to get the most and threatening every other
dog that comes near them. The clever ones grab the

best bits in sight and run off with them, while the clumsy ones allow themselves to be pushed about till suddenly they find their back feet in the still-red ashes of the recently dumped stove. It's no place for any but a wise and active dog.

When the moving is over there is not much to show that a camp was ever there. One will see an oval arrangement of stones, the size of a man's head or larger, which held down the edges of the tent and, in most cases, a line of smaller stones stretching from one side to the other near the middle of the oval, marking the edge of the sleeping area. These tent-rings are dotted all along the Arctic coast line, wherever the Eskimos have been, and are valuable guides to the archæologist, for their presence means that here was a camping place and that igloo remains may well be expected in the same vicinity.

Now that *The Tiger* was ready to cast off, Bobby found himself homeless, so he decided that this was a good time to attempt the crossing to the Button Islands. We in our turn, therefore, loaded all our goods and chattels on board our motor-boat and started out.

Between our camp and the outer fringe of islands lay an incredibly beautiful bay. Bare, gaunt, rocky shores spattered here and there with green, yellow, red; sparkling blue water, with a million points of light glittering in the sun glade, flashing from every ripple; blue, cloudless sky— all this, save for the absence of tree or bush, might have been duplicated on any one of ten thousand lakes in the Canadian north woods. What gave the scene its unique interest was a fleet of twenty or more kayaks, each carrying its seal hunter, his paddle flashing in the sun, moving easily over the surface, now this way, now that, avoiding the occasional block of floating ice, ever on the alert for the round black head of a seal.

The noise of our motor drowned out almost all other

sounds till Bobby, picking up his rifle, installed himself in the bows and signalled to Davidee to switch off the ignition so that we might drift quietly and, perhaps, get a shot at a seal ourselves. It was then that the last perfecting touch was added to the scene. To my surprise and delight, I found that many of the men were singing to themselves as they paddled along. It was entirely unaffected, almost unconscious; a simple, natural expression of contentment with themselves, the weather, with their world as they knew it. Nor were these the hymns of the mission, but rather the old songs of the Eskimos themselves.

To-day, whenever my thoughts are brought back to the North by some chance word or sight, it is to this smiling, sun-lit bay that my mind turns, and to the men who sang as they hunted for their food in its waters.

Bobby had explained to me that he intended to cross Gray Straits just when the tide was on the turn and that, in order to do this, we should arrive at the outer islands about an hour before slack water. We had some time to spare now, and hunting was as good a way to fill it as any other. We drifted with the current but, by bad luck, no seals broke surface near enough for a shot. Soon it was time to start our motor again and take up our position ready for the crossing, at the lee side of one of the islands.

Even in this remote spot we found a small camp, two tents pitched on the beach of a sheltered cove. We were invited into one of them for a mug-up by a pleasant-faced Eskimo woman, who wore a pair of silver-rimmed spectacles which gave her an air of sedate respectability. She was at work scraping the hair off a seal skin with a steel *ulu*. This knife she kept sharp with a whetstone of which she made frequent use, for an *ulu* must be sharp as a razor for this job. After whetting the blade, she finished the edge by rubbing it with a large steel needle. Another woman, working with her, had the habit of stropping her *ulu*, after whetting it, on the leg of her sealskin boot.

The hair which comes off in this process of scraping does not appear to be used for any purpose, but it is gathered up carefully as it is shaved off and laid in a shallow tin, or in a frying-pan, to prevent its getting all over the bedding and into the food. The skin is limp from being soaked in water and the hair clots together in little windrows.

When Bobby judged that the tide was right we slipped out of our shelter and rounded a rocky point. There before us lay Gray Straits, smoother than usual but not dead calm, with a steady procession of icebergs and smaller bits of pan ice sailing along with the tide.

Clear and sharp in the crystal air, about four miles off to the north, we could see our goal, the Button Islands, so named in honour of Sir Thomas Button who sailed from England in May, 1612, in command of two ships, the *Resolution* and the *Discovery*. He crossed Hudson Bay on that trip and wintered on its western shore.

As long as the islands were in sight all was well, for we could see where we were headed for but, even as we stared at them and before we were even a quarter of the way across, their outlines grew dim, fog drifted over the straits, and they were hidden from us.

Quickly we glanced back. The main island of Killinek was still in sight, but it too was rapidly being obscured by thin veils of mist and soon only the tops of the highest cliffs, towering some fourteen hundred feet above us, were visible. Reluctantly, but with no loss of time, we turned back, for it would have been foolhardy to attempt to raise the islands guided by my compass alone with such strong currents and changeable tides running; if we delayed in turning back we might well lose sight of our one remaining link with known waters.

On approaching the land again, we stopped our motor and lay idle for half an hour or so, hoping for a possible improvement in the weather, but it was soon evident that things were getting worse, rather than better, and we were obliged to return to our original camp. Bobby and Davidee both wore rather long faces and our disappointment was keen enough, but, when we once more hauled ashore my little tent, and started to put it up on the same old spot, the humour of the situation struck us all.

"*Koukput!*" Bobby lifted his right leg into a swinging stamp and struck his fist into the palm of his hand, as he shouted the word.

"To-morrow!" we all agreed, determined to make it next time.

Towards dusk I was invited into the tent where Davidee had taken up temporary quarters and here I was offered my first seal-meat. I had had several meals of the liver and, though I liked it well enough, it was just beginning to pall. The meat itself I had not yet tried.

As a rule the Eskimo eat their meat boiled or stewed, and there is nearly always a pot-full simmering on top of the stove or over the soapstone *koodlee* or lamp, if they have no stove. When a man comes in hungry, he helps himself to what is in the pot, and the woman of the household sees to it that it is kept filled. The thick rich soup which results from this perpetual stock pot is a favourite, and most nourishing, drink.

Seal-meat, before cooking as well as after it, is dark in colour, rubbery in appearance, and not particularly appetizing. Its taste, however, is very good. It didn't remind me specially of beef, or of pork, or of any other meat with which we are familiar, but it's excellent food and will soon fill a hungry man. The Eskimo, if deprived

" Soon another family arrived "

"Not much care had been taken in the construction of the grave"

of seal-meat, soon feels a great hunger for it and, for him, there is nothing that will take its place. He finds it hard to believe that there is no seal-meat in the land where the white man comes from. How can one live in such a country?

Once again I began my prowling about, more as a means of keeping busy than in the expectation of finding anything of great importance. However, I did come across a large, though broken, cooking-pot, similar in shape to the one the two women had given me a day or two before. It was stuck upon a sharp pinnacle of rock, just as a lost glove may be seen on a picket in a fence. I added it to my already growing collection in a discarded sugar-box.

Late the next morning, Bobby suggested that we make a second attempt. We set out once more across the bay where the singing hunters were paddling their kayaks, and again we stopped at the little camp on the outer island and had another mug-up with the respectable-looking person with the spectacles who had now finished her skin scraping and was sewing a pair of *kamiks*. Once more, when the time was ripe, we slipped through a narrow gut between two islands and out into the straits.

Again the Button Islands were in sight, though not as sharp and clear as they had been. There was a "loom" hovering above them, as the Newfoundlanders call it, or a mirage. The islands themselves were there right enough, but above them shimmered a second image of themselves, upside down, and connected with the actual islands by slender columns of mirage. Such optical effects are very frequent in the North; in some cases the reversed image reflects objects which cannot actually be seen because they are hidden by the curve of the earth's surface, and sometimes ice conditions many miles away can be foretold by the mirage.

F

This time there was no ice in sight, no fog, and very little swell. Our plan of campaign was to start out steering north-west, against the tide, which was flowing towards the east. This combination of movements would carry us approximately straight north. When the tide turned, we should be half-way over and then, as the tide reversed its direction, we would turn our bows to the north-east to counteract it, and still be carried north, and in this manner we hoped to maintain a steady course towards the shelter of the islands. The motor-boat was to lead and tow Bobby's sailboat, while he was to hoist his sail so as to take advantage of any wind there might be and thus lessen the drag on the motor.

In spite of the better weather, the mainland was quite out of sight before we were more than half-way. The water was smooth enough now that it was near slack tide; at its full it boils along at a rate of six knots. Not far ahead of us we could see a line of creamy white. It was a vast tide-rip, harmless enough to all appearances till we were right on top of it and then we saw that it was a wide lane of troubled waters, tossing violently, running in all directions, spinning into sudden whirlpools, now smoothing itself for a moment into oily calms, then boiling up again in anger as though trying to catch us off our guard.

Wildly we rocked and pitched. There was nothing any of us could do but to sit and watch, hope the motor would not die, hope no sudden strain on the tow rope would part it, for it would slack off suddenly and threaten to wrap itself round the propeller and then jerk taut again, twanging like a bow-string and snapping off thousands of glittering droplets. Everything held firm and the motor steadily throbbed its way along, across the roaring tide-rip, into the smoother waters beyond. Here, its vital task accomplished, it stopped dead.

Currents and eddies were still all about us and there was danger of our being carried on to a near-by reef. Bobby, seeing what had happened, held a steady course ahead with a full sail, took us in tow and hauled us clear. It was a good example of his precise thinking and quick action.

Having adjusted the spark, the cause of our motor's failure, we cruised along till we gained the lee of the westward islands. Here there was no hint of any wind. A bright sun shone down upon us and the still air was warm and pleasant. We steered northwards between the scattered islands, pausing once to investigate a little bay which was known to be a good place for seals. Nothing there, so we continued on our way.

There are two principal islands in the group, MacColl and Lawson, each about six miles long and a mile and a half wide. They lie parallel and run from south-west to north-east. Between them lies a narrow, straight channel, half a mile wide, littered with loose ice, and strewn with reefs and rocks awash. Bobby and Davidee both knew it well and showed no hesitation.

Our goal was Lacy Island, a smaller body of land at the extreme north-east corner of the group. Bobby had camped here before, only the previous year in fact, and knew that there were old igloo ruins to be seen there as well as at another place near by. We had still seven or eight miles to go before reaching "home."

The shores of the islands are bold and upright and, for the most part, devoid of vegetation. An occasional snow bank still lay on the shady side of a hill. Along high-water mark ran a curious band of colours: green, cream and black. The lowest band, the green one, was due to a coating of small seaweeds which found a precarious foothold on the smoothly polished rock. Most of the time this band is under water and it is visible only when the tide is low. Next in order, the cream-coloured line, was the bare rock itself, scraped clear of all growth of any kind by the scouring of the spring break-up, when cakes of ice rush pell-mell through the narrow channels grinding and crushing themselves to powder as they run. Above this raw scar was a line of black lichens which seem to thrive best on rocks which are frequently washed over by salt water. Not only does this band of colours give a bright and gay appearance to the shore line, but it serves to tell at a glance the state of the tide.

Above our heads, gulls wheeled and soared and Mark, glancing up at them, scrambled across from the sailboat which, now that we were in safe waters, had drawn up alongside ours. With him he carried a ramshackle old ·22 rifle. He shot several of the young gulls and, as they fell into the water ahead of us, Davidee would steer the boat towards them to let Bobby snatch the birds out with the boat-hook. Two of the first he threw across to Jenny who immediately skinned them and cut off the wings.

Calling to little Jimmy, who was lying wrapped up snug and warm in the loose folds of the lowered sail, she took off his little boy's *kamiks*, turned the two gull skins inside out and slipped them on his feet. Jimmy wiggled his toes proudly in his new socks and resumed his boots. The bodies of the birds were laid aside for food and the wings were kept to use as brushes, just as turkey's wings used to be used for cleaning the top of the stove in the old farm kitchen.

Later on in that warm and glowing afternoon we came to the end of the long narrow channel between the islands and saw the wide open expanse of Hudson Strait before us. Turning into the shelter of a horseshoe bay we drew alongside some convenient rocks and went ashore.

We were there!

On the Buttons, at last. Notorious Gray Straits had been conquered and we could get to work.

Our new camp site was not unlike the old one except that the peninsula, which here also ended in a spit of rocks from which one might shoot seals, was larger than the other had been and, instead of being bare rock, was fairly well covered with turf and flowers.

A little way inland was a ridge of coarse gravel, about twenty-five feet above sea-level and on this two ruined igloos could easily be distinguished.

Leaving the others to unload the equipment, for I was too impatient to stay and help them, I went up to investigate. Too fresh and green to be very old, I decided, but this was only the beginning: there might be others. Sure enough, still farther inland, and this time about fifty feet above the sea, were two more. True, they didn't look any older but, as the two pairs of houses were at different distances from, and heights above, the sea, I was justified in hoping that they might prove to be of different ages. I decided that, if I found no better ones, I would excavate one of each pair, so that I might compare their contents.

Jenny called and waved to me, asking where my tents were to be pitched. Reluctantly I turned back. After all, I reflected, these igloos had been waiting for me a good many years. Surely they could wait till to-morrow!

Chapter VII

OUR CAMP ON THE BUTTON ISLANDS

BOBBY knew just where he was going to pitch his tent, for he had camped here before, but the choice of suitable spots was limited. All the stretches of ground covered with vegetation of any sort were very wet, there were but few gravelly spots, and tent pegs can never hold in rocky soil. Eventually we found a little rise of ground which seemed somewhat drier than the rest and it was here that I decided to place my sleeping tent. My work tent would be put up the next morning, near by.

There are decided advantages to having two tents when one is travelling by boat and expecting to camp for some time in one spot. The extra weight of a second tent is an unimportant item under such circumstances, whereas if one were back-packing it might be out of the question. Then, too, if one's camps are for a day or so only, it would be foolish to go to the trouble of setting up two tents.

In my present case, however, the additional work tent meant that I could leave all my "office" paraphernalia scattered about at night when I went to bed—in the other tent. I could do all my recording and writing, my numbering and wrapping of specimens in the larger tent which measured eight by ten feet, as well as what cooking Jenny left for me to look after, and meanwhile I could have my folding cot standing and ready for use in the smaller "silk" tent, which was seven by nine. It saved putting endless things away each morning and evening.

Fresh water had been one of the things which I was somewhat concerned about, for I was not sure how permanent or how good the supply might be. I need have had no worry on that score, for Lacy Island, and every inch of solid land for many miles about us, was continuously drenched with rain. There was a healthy little brook trickling down from the gravel terraces where the old igloos lay, and it gathered in a little pool lined with sphagnum moss, only a few yards from my tent.

From here the brook proceeded down to the beach which it struck at a point where there was a little cliff, perhaps twelve feet high. Down this it cascaded in a miniature waterfall, springing free and clear. Near by was a convenient ledge where one could stand and hold a bucket under the waterfall, filling it in a few minutes or in a moment, depending on the immediate state of the supply. After a heavy rainstorm, it would take but an instant to fill a pail, but after a couple of days of dry weather, one might have to wait five or ten minutes before the diminutive trickle filled it up.

In one of these drought periods, Jenny got an old tin can which I had discarded and bent it into a little trough. This she wedged into a crevice in the rocks, so disposed as to divert the water into a course a few inches from its previous one. Now she could stand the pail on a rocky shelf and leave it to fill itself. Little Jimmy was much impressed with this ingenious arrangement and frequently attempted to improve on it, usually with no success whatever, and many indignant protests from Jenny.

Near the edges of the little stream the moss grew thick and dense. While walking near this on the evening of our arrival, I was surprised to see a series of deep depressions, where the moss had been pressed down by a heavy foot so that the green of the upper part of the moss was forced aside and the brown of the lower sections could be seen. A little puddle of water had gathered in each one, and the water was still muddy.

"Bobby!" I called.

Bobby was down at his own tent, nearly a hundred yards away. He looked up from a large stone he was rolling into position to make a guy rope fast to, and came over to see what I was pointing at.

"*Nanook?*" I asked, showing him the tracks, for I felt that a polar bear was the only possible author.

"*Nanook!*" agreed Bobby excitedly, and Mark and Davidee came running up in answer to his shout. The three of them examined the tracks carefully, noted which way the animal had gone and, as far as I could make out, were of the opinion that it was a bear of about two years of age which had been there so recently that it had probably been disturbed by our arrival. It would soon be dusk, or they would have gone after it, I feel sure, even if the tracks would be difficult to follow once it left the soft moss and grass for hard rock.

Jenny and Lily were plainly alarmed. The polar bear is one animal the women are definitely afraid of. The men will attack one wherever and whenever it is seen if they have any weapons with which it can possibly be vanquished, for they are bold and courageous hunters. Nevertheless, they have the greatest appreciation of, and respect for, Nanook's ability as a fighter, ferocious, cunning and relentless.

While we were standing by the side of the mossy little stream, discussing the tracks and chatting quietly in the still evening air, puffing on our cigarettes, Jenny absently bent down and pulled up a handful of the sphagnum growing so abundantly at our feet. She squeezed the water from it, and fluffed out the ball of green moss in her hands. This, still listening to what was being said, she laid on a bare rock near by, then another beside it, and another, and another. Lily began to do the same thing, pulling, squeezing, fluffing, till a couple of dozen handfuls had been gathered.

These were left to dry somewhat and were taken into the tent for a final drying a couple of days later, when rain appeared imminent. Sphagnum moss has a multitude of uses among Eskimo women. It makes excellent diapers for the infants, easily disposable, inexpensive, sanitary, possessing all the virtues of the most extensively advertised equivalents that we have. After the girls reach maturity they still find it invaluable and use it regularly. So useful and efficient is sphagnum moss that a number of white women in the North, deprived of the materials available to their southern sisters, take a leaf from the books of the Eskimo girls and use it themselves. At the trading posts and missions, old catalogues may still grace the rear premises; in remoter districts and in camp, sphagnum moss is regulation equipment, and nobody finds any fault with it.

It was with considerable relief that I crawled at last into my warm and comfortable sleeping bag, which now no longer reposed on wet and rocky ground, but on a folding camp-cot. Usually I find it difficult to sleep in strange surroundings, but not this time. I was dead tired, not so much from physical exertion, though there had been plenty of that, as from mental tension.

It was a reasonably formidable undertaking, this crossing of Gray Straits in a small motor-boat. We had all known that there were risks of one sort and another: sudden bad weather, a faulty engine which might die and let the tide carry us far out into the Atlantic, or an upset in a bad tide-rip. We had ventured all these and had come through unscathed, and there was a definite sense of accomplishment and relief. Sleep was welcome and came easily, and the alarm clock rang for a long time the next morning before I stretched out a sleepy arm to shut it off.

Bright warm sunlight, a light breeze, the cries of a thousand gulls greeted me. Right opposite our camp site on Lacy Island lay Goodwin Island and on the side facing us rose sheer cliffs where the gulls nest and rear their young. All day long they came and went from their breeding-cliffs and, when the wind was right, the sound of their ceaseless talk was carried to us, while their white wings glinted when the sunlight caught the glistening feathers.

Jenny met me with something to eat. I forget what now, but in those first few days meals were pretty sketchy. There were so many things to do, so much more interesting and pressing than eating. One of them was unexpected, on my part at any rate.

What with going and coming from the sealing camp to the outpost and back again and never knowing what might happen next in the way of a chance to cross the Straits, I had not shaved for two or three days and my face was peppered with a black and vigorous stubble.

Jenny eyed this growth with displeasure and went through the motions of shaving. She didn't actually say, " It's time you had a shave, you look like hell! " but it was clear enough that that was what was in her mind. Now, normally I am not henpecked, nor does my wife tyrannize unduly over me or my doings. Seldom, if ever, has she found it necessary to suggest that I shave, but here was Jenny taking on the duties of a comic-strip wife!

I shaved.

Jenny never had occasion to remind me again.

Little Jimmy had been watching the operation with great interest, for he had probably never seen a man shaving before. Eskimo men have very little hair on their faces and do not find it necessary to shave. Old men get a few scraggly whiskers and even middle-aged men may develop a moustache; some half-breeds are just as hairy as white men. What fascinated Jimmy was my shaving mirror. I took it down from the tent pole where I had tied it and let him look at himself in it. The glass was flat on one side and concave on the other and he turned from the image of "Jimmy *mikiuk*" back to "Jimmy *angiuk*" again and again. What made one side show "Little Jimmy" and the other "Big Jimmy"? It was a problem which baffled him even till the last day, when he saw me packing up my things and begged for a last look at the puzzling mirror.

As soon as Bobby had had breakfast, he came again and asked permission to use the motor-boat for seal hunting. We had tried for a seal the day before when first we got into the lea of the Button Islands, but had had no luck, and now there was no meat left.

Soon he and Davidee were heading out in the direction of Goodwin Island to a bay where they knew seals might be expected. It had been my intention to send the motor-boat back to the Post as soon as I was established, but the fresh breeze from the west and the conditions of the water outside the shelter of the island as seen through my binoculars were indication enough that it would be much too rough to try crossing the straits that day.

Jenny and I set out for a more careful examination of our surroundings than had been possible the evening before. There didn't appear to be any more igloos in the vicinity and, as a matter of fact, we never did find any more anywhere on Lacy Island. On the rocky hillsides about the camp we did find a number of graves and it was evident that they were recent.

Those graves which we had found near the sealing camp a few days before had had grave goods concealed near them, but these graves had quite large articles placed right up on top of them. Two graves were crowned by the wooden frames of kayaks and another bore the remains of a large wooden sled. Sad to say nearly all the graves in the immediate vicinity had been rifled by some irresponsible person and the kayak frames had been wantonly broken and scattered.

"*Kablunah!*" exclaimed Bobby, when I showed him these that evening, with a grimace.

"White men!" Of course. Who else? No Eskimo would do such a thing. Not because any feeling of reverence would restrain them, but simply because they are not impelled by that strange urge to smash and break things, that overpowering drive towards vandalism that seems to afflict so many white men of lesser intelligence. Scattered among the rocks here and there was tell-tale evidence—the black paper tabs pulled out and torn off from their film-pack cameras! I hope the photographs were taken before the graves were disturbed and that they were deposited in some permanent collection.

On our way back to the tents, Jenny and I came across a number of puff-balls, each about an inch in diameter and with firm white flesh. I picked one or two of them and asked Jenny if they were accustomed to eat them. At any rate, that is what I tried to say. Actually I had to rely on extemporized sign language.

She expressed surprise, distaste, and a definitely negative answer. Later I was told that the Eskimos never eat them and, while they may not consider them harmful, have certainly never thought of them as edible. I knew that puff-balls are edible as long as their flesh is firm and felt quite sure that I might eat them in safety, but caution or cowardice overcame my theoretical confidence. I was altogether too far from a doctor and a stomach pump to take any chances.

The Eskimo has a number of curious avoidances. So have we for that matter, but we are familiar with our own foibles and take them for granted. Bumble bees, for instance, fill the Eskimo soul with terror of a voltage considerably higher than the circumstances seem to warrant. Just why this should be, I have no idea, but the bee certainly appears to be looked upon as something more than a common and insignificant insect. These people make frequent use of charms, both to prevent sickness and to cure it, as well as for a great variety of other purposes, and bees are not infrequently enclosed in small wooden boxes, or in little pockets of leather or cloth, alive of course, so that their energy and fierceness may work in magical ways.

They seem, too, to fear the little red mites which are common in fresh water and will carefully strain these out before drinking. So would we, no doubt, but with much less show of concern.

All who have travelled in northern Canada or in the Arctic will join heartily in condemning the mosquito as the worst plague the country can offer. In summer they are present in incredible numbers and they are filled with a most phenomenal voracity. Champlain cursed them on the St. Lawrence many, many years ago and so has everybody else, both before him and since. One early explorer, Captain Richard Whitbourne, who was in Newfoundland in 1615, tried to find relief for his feelings in humour and says, in the conclusion of his *Discourse and Discovery of Newfoundland Trade*:

Those Flies seem to haue a great power and authority vpon all loytering people that come to the New-Found-Land: for they haue this property, that when they finde any such lying lazily, or sleeping in the Woods, they will presently bee more nimble to seize on them, than any Sargeant will bee to arrest a man for debt: Neither will they leaue stinging or sucking out the blood of such sluggards, vntill, like a Beadle, they bring him to his Master, where hee should labour: in which time of loytering, those Flies will so brand idle persons in their faces, that they may be known from others, as the Turkes doe their Slaues.

After lunch, the good weather and bright sunlight still holding, I took photographs of the four igloos or, rather, of three of them, for one was already in the shadow of the steep hill which loomed just behind our camp. Here and there in the grass were bits of white man's gear, and my feeling that these were recent houses was strengthened. Nevertheless, the fact that they had been occupied since the first coming of white explorers and whalers need not prevent their having been used in earlier days too. Only excavation would tell us what they had to reveal.

Lily had wandered along the beach in search of driftwood to burn in the stove. We had picked up a few good pieces on our way from Port Burwell, but there was always a need for more. We watched her as she strolled along quite unaware that she was observed, picking her nose and wiping her fingers on a convenient rock and then on her dress, stooping now and then to pick up some small fragment of wood which she placed, for convenience in carrying it, in the hood of her parka as it hung down from the back of her neck.

Apparently one of the most deeply rooted fallacies concerning the Eskimo is the belief that the women carry their children in the hoods of their parkas. This is not so and the mothers are always much amused when asked about it. Babies are carried on the mother's back, stark naked as a rule except for a little cap of wool or fur. When a child is in this position he can peer out from the edge of the opening over his mother's shoulder and a careless observer gets the impression that the child is crouched in the hood itself. The women make their parkas with a special enlargement on the back to accommodate the child; a belt and straps in front take the strain off the mother's throat and neck.

The word *parka* is Russian rather than Eskimo and was used to designate a hoodless smock-like garment reaching from the neck to the knees. When the first Russian traders and explorers crossed Bering Straits and found the Eskimos wearing such garments (though with a hood) they called them parkas after the article familiar to them, and the name stuck. In quite recent years, hoods for use in cold weather have appeared on the market in Canada and the United States and such hoods are now referred to as parkas, because they resemble the hood on the Eskimo "parkas," in ignorance of the fact that the true parka (of the Russian) had no hood at all.

Out on the rocky spit, near Bobby's tent, Mark sat in the lee of a little windbreak waiting patiently for a seal to show itself. He had not gone with Bobby and Davidee, possibly because Jenny thought the polar bear might still be somewhere around and it was just as well to have somebody at hand who was accustomed to dealing with such animals. I wasn't, and she knew it.

Little Jimmy was playing by himself. He was an indefatigable child. Nearly always he played alone, for he was the only youngster in the family and they might be weeks at a time without seeing any other people.

Usually he played quietly and seriously, making up all sorts of little games and employments for himself. If anybody passed by near enough for him to shout at them, he would call loudly.

"*Atata!*" he would cry to his father. "*Atata! Tukko!*" "Father! Look!" and he would fling a stone into the water, so that his father might praise him for his skill.

"*Anana!*" was his mother, and he would call to her in just the same way, till he had secured her attention and then perform some feat for her edification. Always they would watch and applaud him, making some little remark to assure him that he had been seen and his skill observed.

He was quite used to me by this time and we went down to the beach together for a few minutes. I picked up some flat stones and made them skip along the top of the water, playing ducks and drakes. He was highly delighted and urged me to do it again and again. He tried it too, but could not understand that the stone had to be thrown so that the flat side struck the water. Always his would hit edge on and sink with a defeated plop, while mine hopped gaily along the top. Whether this amusement is familiar to the Eskimos or not, Bobby and Mark both were successful when we all tried it another day.

There was no regular bed-time for little Jimmy, though he generally slept when the older members of his family did. Eskimo children are much less governed by the clock than are ours and they go to sleep when they are tired, eat when they are hungry, and play as long as they are awake. At all hours of the long summer night, one can hear the voices of children playing if there are enough people camped together to make a little village. It is a pleasant sound, for the voices of children at a distance

"The watch for seals is constant and unremitting"

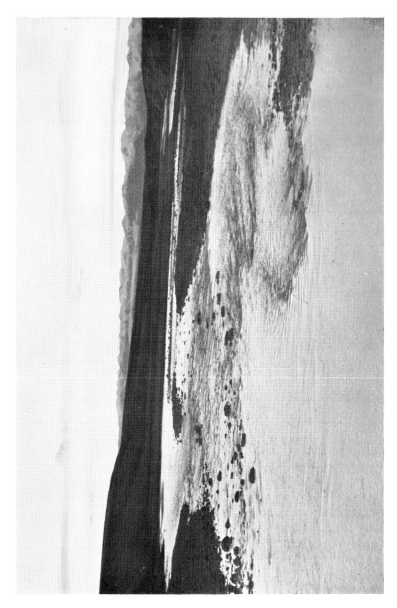

"This is a land of very rapid run-off"

in still air have a clear pure quality which lingers long in one's memory.

They are completely unrestrained in their play. Modern pedagogues with theories of unrepressed egos would find much to reflect upon down North. Nobody says "Don't" unless the occasion is serious, dangerous, or very annoying, as when a scrambling child, eager to get out of the tent to take part in some fun or other, brings the tent pole down. This happens every now and then, and the grown-ups patiently put the pole back into position, remonstrating with the urchin, but never thinking of slapping him or punishing him in any other way.

So unrestrained are they in their play that they grow up with a much better knowledge of what we euphemistically call the "facts of life" than most of our own children possess, even after the bees and the flowers have been explained to them. There isn't much they haven't found out from observation and experiment. Nobody worries. Nobody objects. Nobody comes to any harm.

Nevertheless, when one is lying sleepless at night, and continuous calls and shouts from a vigorous football game pierce the midnight air, one does wish that Eskimo children would share the nature of older human beings and, at least occasionally, go to bed!

That evening I got a Coleman lantern going in my work tent and set up my folding table and other stuff. I was writing my notes and doing other office chores which are a tedious but necessary part of expeditions of this kind, when I heard Bobby and the others talking outside.

The motor-boat had returned towards evening with two fine seals, and Lily and Jenny, or rather Jenny and Lily, had been at work on them. Now all that was done, everybody was fed and at peace and it was time for a visit and an enquiry into what the white man was up to.

They came in and disposed themselves on boxes and whatever else was available and waited.

Conversation was out of the question, for I couldn't talk to them and it would have been rude, they felt, for them to carry on a discourse in their own language. I grinned amiably, and they did the same.

It was Jenny who solved the impasse.

With a quick "*'Tsiro!*" she jumped to her feet and slipped out of the tent. That "*'Tsiro!*" bothered me for weeks. It was not to be found in the dictionary I had with me. Once I repeated it to Jenny with a rising inflection, as much as to say "What's this *'Tsiro* business?" but she merely looked mystified. Eventually I discovered it was an abbreviation of a longer word, *uvatsearo*, which means "Just a minute."

Well, in just a minute or a little less, Jenny was back with a loop of sinew cord and we worked at cat's cradles for the rest of the evening. She was amazingly clever at them. One after another she would produce new and extraordinary shapes, often of the most intricate kind.

Bobby and Mark merely looked on, and so did Davidee. Men don't like that kind of thing. It's not wise to get your fingers and thumbs all tangled up in strings and cords. It might happen once too often. Just when you had harpooned a seal, perhaps, and then your thumb might get a loop of rawhide thong round it and be pulled right off. No! Better keep away from that sort of thing.

Later on, when it was getting late and I was ready for bed, I had no idea of the polite formula which would bring the evening to an end. At last, I turned enquiringly to Jenny and asked "Tea?"

"*Ee!*" she answered quickly. "*Oovunga.*" She left the tent and went to her own to boil the water for tea. *Oovunga* simply means "I, myself" and she had meant that she would make tea for all of us. Soon she was back with a large pot of it, hot, strong, and black; we all drank heartily, and so to bed.

Nearly all the work of the camp seemed to fall on Jenny's competent shoulders. While Lily was, strictly, the chatelaine of Bobby's household, it was Jenny who actually did most of the work, for it would never have been done otherwise. To a casual observer there would have appeared to be a good deal of truth in the old belief that native women do all the work while the men loaf about if not off somewhere or other hunting and fishing. This is far from the true situation, of course, for among the Eskimos, as among ourselves, men and women each have their separate spheres of action and daily duties. The men hunt and fish, true enough, but hunting and fishing are not mere sport or recreation, as they are with us, but urgent affairs, nearly always onerous, usually fatiguing, and frequently dangerous. The proportion of Eskimo men who live to an old age is small, for many of them die a violent death as a result of some accident which occurs while they are hunting or fishing, or travelling to or from the hunting-grounds.

In addition to the duty of providing food for the family, the men keep their weapons and tools in repair, make their kayaks and sleds, provide food for the dogs, which is often a more burdensome task than feeding the family, and, when necessary, protect the women and children from assaults from men or animals. Theirs, too, is the task of building the shelter which protects them all from the inclement winter weather.

The women's duties are the household cares of women the world over. Cooking the food provided by the men, caring for the children, making and mending clothes, tending the fire or lamp, skinning the game and preparing it for the pot. All these duties, while they go on for ever and are never finished, are lighter than the men's work and considerably less dangerous.

Jenny was, perhaps, somewhat busier than usual for she had a good deal of the work in Bobby's tent to look after, she did most of the cooking for me and, in her spare moments, she helped me in the excavating, a job at which she soon became quite skilful and which she enjoyed much more than any of her other tasks.

She had the instincts of a good housekeeper and liked to see things kept straight. On one occasion she apologized for some disorder in Bobby's tent, more apparent to me than to her for it was usually a fairly astonishing litter. I assured her, in my broken Eskimo jargon, that I quite understood, that in a tent one was apt to let things slide, whereas in a house everything would be kept in much better order. "*Eeee!*" she agreed, with some enthusiasm, evidently impressed with the completeness of my understanding.

To the stranger, the average Eskimo summer tent does indeed present a scene of very obvious disorder. In the first place, the floor is usually merely coarse gravel, sand, and a few random larger stones, only the very biggest ones having been thrown out before erecting the tent. Most of the canvas tents used in the eastern Arctic are oval in shape, having two vertical poles connected by a short ridge pole. The stove is near the front tent pole, and the front edge of the sleeping platform comes as far forward as the rear tent pole.

This sleeping "platform" is called such by courtesy only, in most tents. Its front limits may be marked by a pole stretched across, or merely by the ends of the various skins and blankets on and under which the people sleep. The beds are never "made," in our sense of the expression, being used in the daytime as a sort of divan on which to snooze or to sit while eating or working. Once in a week or so, if the weather is fine, the bedding may be dragged out for an airing and then replaced more or less in order.

The modern canvas tents are usually made with a wall a couple of feet high, and against this wall stand several boxes and skin bags. Those at the sleeping platform end of the tent will contain spare clothing, sewing outfits, personal trinkets, and odds and ends belonging to the women. Other objects, at the sides of the tent, will be the men's tool boxes, bundles of hides either in process of preparation or stored for making clothes or boots, and spare equipment of one sort and another.

Near the stove will be pots and pans, a cup or two, a tea kettle if it is not on the top of the stove, bits of wood gathered on the beach to be used as fuel, a few bones if the dogs haven't been in recently, some dead fish, bits of meat and strips of old blubber, a knife or two, and anything else which happens to be lying about on the ground from a baby's sealskin boot to a Prayer Book in syllabic script.

There is usually a definite smell to all this miscellaneous rubbish, a smell which lingers on the air and in the memory long and persistently. It, like most smells, is quite indescribable but, like Brooke's river-smell, "unforgettable, unforgotten." When first encountered, it is often felt to be an overpowering stench, but one soon becomes accustomed to it and, years later perhaps, on opening a museum storage case, a whiff of it brings back old memories and a keen nostalgia.

Most Eskimo clothing has this powerful aroma about

it, for seal oil gets into everything, especially work clothes and, when it becomes rancid, there is no escaping. Then, too, the people seldom bathe, if ever, and their diet is very largely meat. However, the Eskimos all agree that the average white man smells pretty sour to them, so it's not all one sided!

Chapter VIII

FROZEN HOUSES

THE motor-boat had been waiting for fine weather to
get back to Port Burwell, where many jobs awaited
its return. I had intended sending it back the day
after we reached the Islands, but it had been too rough
and so I had postponed its departure for another day.

This morning the weather looked much more favour-
able. Through the field glasses we could see an occasional
white cap off to sea, showing that it was not a dead calm
outside, or anything like it. It seldom is down North.
Davidee shook hands all round, not forgetting little
Jimmy, and climbed aboard. Without a hitch, the motor
started and in a few minutes she was out of sight. He
had twenty gallons of petrol, a full day to do it in, and
fair weather. It was weeks later that we heard that he
had met with strong winds and bad water and nearly
didn't "make it."

And now I was alone with my adopted family. We
were still comparative strangers to each other and the
language offered serious difficulties. Something of the
same thought must have been born in Bobby's brain at
the same time for, as I glanced at him, I saw he was
staring meditatively at me. He looked so serious that I
had to smile. Immediately he did so too.

"*Peeouyuk?*" I enquired.

"*Eee! Peeouyuk!*" he answered at once, "sure, everything's fine."

So that was all right, and we turned our backs on the sea and walked towards the ruined igloos.

There are several things that have to be done before one can begin the actual digging in archæological field work. The first, obviously enough, is to make a complete record of the condition of the site before it is disturbed at all.

Photographs have to be taken showing the general appearance of the area, and also of details of every small feature which will later be disturbed. A survey has to be carried out and a map made with everything of importance indicated on it, accurately placed on a convenient scale.

Even when this is finished it is not always possible to go ahead, for consideration has to be given to the question of which features to excavate and which to leave undisturbed so that later archæologists, perhaps with new methods or new information at their disposal, will be able to re-examine the same site and corroborate or, unhappily, confute the conclusions you have arrived at and published.

At this particular site, with two igloos on an upper terrace, about fifty feet above the sea, and two more on another terrace only twenty-five feet up, there was some reason to suppose that the higher pair might be older than the two lower ones, I determined to excavate one of each, leaving the other pair for future investigators to check by.

I had already discovered where the true north lay by marking the position of the Pole Star the night before. Now my compass showed me that the magnetic north was about 45° west of this, for the magnetic pole lies about 1,350 miles south of the true or geographical north pole and about an equal distance north of Winnipeg. It is about 1,133 miles north-west of the Button Islands, whereas the true north pole was still some 2,000 miles due north.

I don't believe that Bobby had, at this stage of the operations, any very concrete picture of what it was I wanted him to help me with when we did reach the Button Islands. He knew that we were in quest of the remains of the "old people," but just what those remains might consist of and how we were to go about finding them must have been somewhat vague in his mind.

Now it became clear that we were to dig into the old house ruins with the shovels and trowels that I had brought with me and the idea appealed to him at once. He was eager to begin, then and there, with good lusty heaves on the shovel handle. It was only by example that I was able to explain that the first step was to strip off the overlying turf from the igloo without disturbing in any way whatever might be found lying just beneath the grass roots.

There was a dense mat of this turf, mingled with brilliant Arctic poppies and purple fireweed, growing inside the ruined walls of the igloo and, by cutting a slit in it and prying up an edge, one could roll back large sections of it, like a thick green carpet.

Immediately under the grass roots were numerous fairly large rocks, weighing fifty pounds or more, which had probably formed part of the roofing, for they lay fair in the middle of the igloo. Rolling them out was hot and tiring work and, when this was done, all the loose soil which had fallen in with the roof, had indeed helped to form it, had to be scraped up and thrown out.

Now came the job of explaining to Bobby and Mark that we had to work systematically in horizontal layers. Their idea of excavating was that each one of my "helpers" including Jenny, Lily and little Jimmy should get a shovel or some other tool and sink a shaft down to bed rock in some private corner.

However, they soon encountered frozen soil and working in horizontal layers was imposed upon them by the force of circumstance. They couldn't work in any other direction. Lily and Jimmy I sent off to their tent, but the other three stayed to help and we soon got rid of the top debris and down to a stratum of earth and rocks with specimens in it.

In that first day we found three fragments of soapstone lamps, a mouthpiece for a bow-drill, a whetstone, the bone tip of a kayak paddle, the ice-pick from the butt end of a harpoon, and altogether twenty-five pieces of one sort and another.

Any one of them might have belonged to a modern Eskimo and they most certainly did not form part of the culture of the "old people" we sought. We spent most of the day at work on this, our first igloo, but the frozen soil and the infrequency of specimens became discouraging towards the end of the afternoon.

Bobby stopped work a little time before the rest of us did and went off in his kayak to try for a seal. He got one in a very few minutes and we all went down to the rocky shore to meet him. Jenny and Lily hauled the carcass up on to a flat ledge to skin it, while the two men took the kayak out of the water, turned it upside down, and rested it in a sheltered place with a couple of large rocks on it to hold it down should the wind get up.

Jenny did most of the actual work, as usual, but this time, as there were only three small dogs to feed, Lily took the small intestines of the seal down to the water's edge instead of including them with the rest of the internal organs for dog feed.

She washed the intestines carefully, squeezing out
the matter which was still in them, and rinsing them
again and again. Next she turned the long red tube
inside out as one would turn the finger of a glove, and
inspected the inner surface carefully. Then she detached
and discarded a long tapeworm, another, and then a
third.

In all probability parasitologists are already familiar
with the particular species of tapeworms which infest
seals, but I have never ceased to regret that I had no
means of preserving these particular specimens.

Lily's next step, having assured herself that the
intestine was now clean and free from visible parasites,
was to make the gut into a chain by forming a loop at
one end and drawing a second loop through it, then
another, and so on to the end. This chain completed, she
draped the looped-up raw entrails over the rocks out of
the reach of the dogs, left it there to dry in the sun, washed
the blood and filth off her hands, and went back to see how
Jenny was progressing.

Dried intestines are a favourite food and, when properly
prepared, are said to be as crisp and tasty as cold bacon.
I have never had an opportunity of trying them, for Bobby
and his family ate up this batch, and no more were made
while I was with them.

It was that evening that I made my first, though by
no means my last, slip in the Eskimo tongue. I had been
working in my tent by the lamplight, writing up my notes
and doing other office chores when, towards ten o'clock,
Jenny came to my tent. She looked about to see if there
was anything that needed doing before she went to
bed.

"*Shinik?*" she enquired. "Sleep?"

In other words, "Are you ready for bed or is there something else you want to do first?"

"*Shinik*," I agreed. "*Shinik mani.*"

Jenny stared fixedly at me, puzzled, then rather angrily.

"*Auka!*" she said firmly. "No!"

What the deuce had I said? Something wrong, sure enough. Then I got it. "*Mani.*" That was it. I had meant to say "Sleep now," but instead of *shinik mana* I had said *shinik mani*, which means not "sleep now," but "sleep here."

Quickly and, I hope, convincingly, I pointed out the similarity between *mani* and *mana* and pleaded my ignorance of the language. I got off with a suspended sentence.

Eskimo is a decidedly tricky language and there are few white men indeed, among the few dozens who can speak it at all, who can speak it like a native. These few are usually people who have been brought up in the North and played with Eskimo children throughout their formative years and have lived there more or less continuously ever since, speaking the language daily with the Eskimos themselves. There are also a few studious missionaries who have made a study of the language, either as part of their duty or by way of a learned recreation.

For the person accustomed to English or any other of the great Indo-European group of languages, it is a difficult tongue indeed and, like many "primitive" languages, by which we usually mean languages spoken by people with a primitive culture, it is incredibly complicated. In an English grammar we can usually get all possible forms of a verb on one page. Not so in Eskimo. One example before me takes fourteen pages of small type, with over six hundred forms in one conjugation alone!

It is a singularly uniform language right from the east coast of Greenland to the western coast of Alaska. In the course of a day or two, any Eskimo from the far east would be able to master the slight differences in the speech of another from the far west, differences principally of pronunciation, stress, and, in some instances, of choice of words.

In the southern part of Alaska, greater linguistic differences begin to make themselves apparent, and on the Aleutian Islands still other changes occur. For a long time students professed themselves unable to relate Eskimo to any language of the Old World, but recent research seems to indicate that it may possibly be related to the Samoyed tongue of Siberia.

If it is true that few white men speak Eskimo, even fewer eastern Eskimos speak English. In the western Arctic the number of English-speaking Eskimos is considerably higher. Bobby had but few words of English. He could say, "Good-bye! O.K. Thank you. How much? Atta boy!" and he knew the names of a few common objects. While he was with me, he never enquired the English name of any article or action, but often instructed me in the proper form in his language.

Jenny, too, was very proud of her ability to count in the white man's language: "One, two, tree, four, funf, sachs, sieben, acht, neun, zehn!" she would chant with glee whenever the opportunity presented itself. She had attended the mission school conducted by Waldmann, the Moravian missionary at Port Burwell, and some of it had stuck.

I don't think Bobby ever knew my name. At first I was simply "*kablunah*"—the white man, or literally "eyebrow." Later I discovered that I had been given a name and it was only after persistent enquiry that I discovered that it was "*tunnitsiuti*"—"he who seeks the Tunnits." I was fortunate! Many of the names hit upon by the Eskimo to distinguish the various white men they know are by no means so inoffensive, and they have a most caustic wit and a keen eye for peculiarities of manner and speech.

There was a missionary in the eastern Arctic, so I am told, who held his nose at an uptilted angle, and, like Queen Elizabeth of old, "walked high and disposedly." There was about his demeanour a vague air of displeasure as though his avocation and his flock were alike offensive to his nostrils. The Eskimos had a name for him. Just how it went in Eskimo, I don't know, but the English of it would be "He who walks as though he sniffed dung."

A day or so after we had settled down it became necessary to move my work tent. I had thought it was on the driest spot in the vicinity, but it soon got very wet indeed, for the water in the vegetation below it seeped up through the floor cloth without any difficulty but was then unable to find a way out, so it lay about in puddles. Jenny and I got busy on the problem, moved all my impedimenta out and, after loosening the guy ropes at the back of the tent, picked the tent and floor cloth up by the rear end and simply poured the water out. Fortunately the weather was warm and sunny and there was but a mild and pleasant breeze.

We had got down to frozen soil in most of the exposed surface of the igloo and I was glad of the hot sun which would thaw things and allow us to go down another few inches.

This perpetually frozen soil is both a boon and a curse to the archæologist in the Arctic. A boon because it preserves things indefinitely as though they had been kept in a giant refrigerator, even feathers and leather being, in some instances, well preserved after long years of burial.

It is a curse too, for it slows down excavation in a way that would drive to the asylum a man with experience in Egypt, used to digging in loose warm sand. Moreover, the frozen soil has a disconcerting habit of allowing you to expose one end of some specimen or other while holding maliciously on at the other end. "Oh, well," you say to yourself, "I'll just leave it there and get it to-morrow when it's thawed out." But you won't, for the soil has another trick up its sleeve and if you fail to cover the exposed end of your specimen up again with a shovelful of soil packed tightly about it, next morning you'll find it in fragments, if it's of bone, ivory, or antler. Apparently the change in temperature as between the two ends introduces stresses and strains beyond its powers of resistance.

However, the sun was out now, and I took the opportunity of drying, numbering, and packing all the specimens collected to date at the sealing camp and from the grave caches. There were one hundred and thirty-eight of them, without counting those collected in the igloo we were working on.

So fine and warm was it that I was able to have lunch out of doors, for all my furniture had been thrown out to allow my tent to dry. Never after that was I to enjoy such a picnic atmosphere, though we ate our lunch out of doors often enough.

At my feet lay Sammy, a short-haired, white-coated beast, the descendant of some dog brought in by a white man. He was not friendly, being unaccustomed to petting and none too trustful of any man who smelt as strange and unfamiliar as I did.

We had two Eskimo dogs with us too, puppies that Bobby had been reluctant to leave behind, fearing they were too young to fend for themselves. They were only a few months old and caused a good deal of trouble at first by running off with any freshly excavated specimen which had been laid aside to dry for a while. More than once I had to dash after them, hurling stones and curses, till the thief dropped his booty, probably in some deep crevice.

They were cross-grained and surly young brutes, quite unwilling to make friends. Port Burwell dogs, I am told, have this unenviable reputation, probably owing to their being cross-bred. Dogs in other parts of the eastern Arctic are said to be affectionate and not dangerous. During the summer months some dogs are ill-fed and there is more than one record of their having attacked people who have stumbled, while feeding them, for instance, and have been killed and eaten. Small infants are never safe where the dogs could possibly get at them.

There was surprisingly little animal life on the Islands, as far as one could see. There were probably foxes, though we saw none, and there must have been lemmings for the foxes to eat. We saw none of these either, though we saw their little haystacks here and there. They are shy and timid creatures and will scuttle out of sight in an instant if alarmed.

Of birds, snow buntings and ravens seemed to be the most conspicuous, with an occasional pipit. At Port Burwell, I noticed white-crowned sparrows, but recorded none on the Buttons.

It is in the sea that life abounds. Strangely enough, microscopic and minute but still visible forms of life are far more numerous in Arctic than in tropical waters. Some areas are more prolific than others and in the quiet and sheltered cove on the shore of which we were camped there was an amazing profusion of marine life.

There were the seals, of course, on which we depended almost entirely for fresh meat. These live largely on crustacea and mollusca and the larger forms of plancton and eat comparatively few fish, of which nevertheless

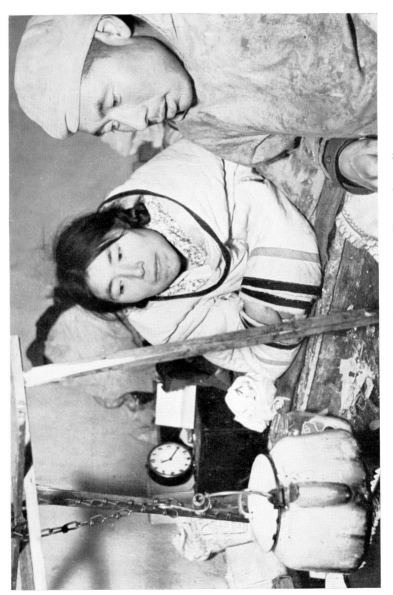

" Simmering over the soapstone koudlee or lamp "

" There are decided advantages to having two tents "

there were many to be had. Cod-fish and Arctic char, sculpins, and many others were abundant. The fish, except for those that are carnivorous, feed on the minute and microscopic life and of this there is a great profusion.

Jellyfish can be seen swimming along in hundreds, pulsing and jerking, opening and closing their umbrellas with an air of unmovable determination which is laughable when one sees how utterly at the mercy of every current they must be. Common, too, are the "blackberries," as the whalers used to call the small black snails which swim along by means of two white wings. They have no shells, snails though they are, and are named pteropods or "wing-feet" on account of their means of progression. They form, small though they are, an important part of the food of whales.

Then there are the swarming millions of creatures so small that they can only just be made out with the naked eye. They are of many kinds and the most diverse habits of life, strange in form, often beautiful in colouring and, to the great majority of men, totally unknown and unthought of, as though they did not exist at all.

Later in the day I moved my work tent to what would, I hoped, prove a drier spot and put all my stuff back inside. There is a definite system for living in a cramped tent, or at any rate there should be such a system. Living without any plan can only lead to trouble whether on the Buttons or in Boston. I was getting things straightened about when Bobby came in asking me to look at his thumb.

Somehow or other he had managed to loosen the nail and the open wound had become infected. There was, also, a boil on his neck and he felt the poison in his thumb was responsible for the boil. The thumb was soon improved by washing with warm water, but the boil wasn't ready for treatment yet. I hesitated to put adhesive tape on the thumb for fear that changing the dressing would

H

take the nail right off, but they do manage to get an ordinary bandage so filthily dirty that one finds it hard to believe that they can possibly escape blood poisoning. Bacteria appear to be few in the North and most cuts and other minor wounds heal up with surprising rapidity and little suppuration.

Mark spent part of the evening shooting from the lookout on the rock point just beyond his tent. He would blaze away at the sleek black head of a breathing seal even when it was far off and there would not have been the slightest chance of recovering it if he hit it. If the people would shoot only when they are reasonably sure of a hit, the seals would probably be less timid and more of them would be secured, and at a less cost in ammunition.

For half an hour or so I joined him with my own rifle, determined not to shoot unless the seal were well within range. Whether it was just bad luck or whether Mark's shooting had frightened them all away, not a seal showed his nose as long as I stayed there.

The next day we determined to investigate MacColl, the more westerly of the two main islands, which lay just about half a mile to the west of our camp. We took Bobby's sailboat, in fact we had no other, and rounded the tip of the island, making a landing on its western side. This was familiar ground to Bobby and he pointed out a little fireplace of stones where he had boiled water for tea several years before. We crossed a narrow, low spit of land, only a few hundred feet, and came out on a beach facing our camp on Lacy Island. Here was a group of four ruined igloos, all at the same level and close together.

Two of these differed somewhat from those with which we were already familiar, for they were rectangular in outline rather than circular, and the walls had been

built up from the ground level, rather than by making
an excavation first and then walling up the sides of it.
These unusual rectangular buildings had a somewhat
recent look about them, for the stones of which the walls
were constructed had less lichens growing on them than
had other stones lying near by which had not been moved
for centuries.

It has been suggested more than once that the slow
growth of these lowly plants might be used as some sort
of a time scale by which to estimate the relative ages of
archæological remains in the Arctic, a thing which would
be useful indeed. But so little that is definite is known
about the rate of growth of lichens and, presumably, so
much depends on such factors as temperature, humidity,
length of winter, hours of sunshine, that we have not yet
been able to do more than say that many lichens on a rock
face suggest that it has been exposed longer than a face
of similar rock that has few or none upon it.

There did not appear to be any graves near these
houses, though there may well have been some farther off
in the hills. There was a shallow pool of unwholesome,
stagnant water near the igloos and, lying in the bottom
of it, were innumerable bones. How deep the bone layer
went we could not tell, but those in sight were enough
to suggest that the site had had either a long history or
a large population.

The freshwater supply for this little village, if it ever
was large enough to deserve that name, came from a
near-by waterfall which now trickled down the face of
the cliff. It was an abrupt and precipitous cliff, about a
hundred feet high, with a curious lip-shaped depression at
its brink, a world too wide for the shrunken stream which
now slipped gently over. At the base of the cliff, below
the waterfall, was a large depression into which that lip
had at one time apparently poured torrents of water. The

edge at the top of the cliff, as we could see by the sunlight glinting on it, was smooth and polished as though from long centuries of pouring.

There was no time to climb to the top of the cliff to see what might be there, but the impression was strong that this was part of an ancient drainage system now no longer functioning on its original scale.

Chapter IX

THE SECOND IGLOO

AFTER we had finished my archæological reconnaissance of MacColl Island, our trip turned into a seal-hunting expedition. It was another fine, warm summer day, the 8th of August. A few hundred feet away to the north-west were the precipitous cliffs of Goodwin Island, on which many birds were nesting. We could hear their continuous cries and see the sun glinting on white wings as they soared and wheeled.

The tide was just on the turn and the arm of the sea between the two islands lay quiet and glittering as light winds stirred its surface. Little ruffles of pattern danced across the water and here and there the round, black head of a seal, like that of a swimming dog, would break the surface. Soon we saw a whole school of them, ten or twelve perhaps, bobbing up and down. Bobby held up his two hands, fingers spread wide apart, moving them up and down alternately, in crude imitation of the movements of the bobbing animals. It is the hunters' signal for a school of seals.

These hunting signals are a well-known feature of Eskimo life. A man, far off on the sky-line perhaps, will stand with his arms stiffly upraised above his head to indicate that he sees caribou, his arms suggesting the great sweeping antlers. Another position, perhaps with one upraised foot, will indicate that he is in reach of a bear, and so on. Thus information is carried over distances

too great to shout across, and there is the other advantage of its being a silent message. So Bobby's reaction
to the sight of the seals and his grin of anticipation
could have but one meaning. He was going out after
them!

He had brought his kayak along, lying on the deck
of the sailboat, and before long he was in it and on his
way. It reminded me of the glittering, sun-lit bay at the
sealing camp, where the men had sung as they paddled
their kayaks, but now Bobby was alone on the water
and he didn't sing this time. He paddled over to
the gull cliff and then let the slow current carry him
gradually back towards us, making no motion with
his paddle, sitting quietly in his kayak with his rifle
ready.

Jenny, Mark and I sat on a big rock which hung over
the water to watch proceedings, while Lily and little
Jimmy started off to investigate the driftwood situation.
Every now and then we would hear Bobby's rifle, but he
had no luck as far as we could see. He was doing better
than we realized, however, for when he got back he had
two seals, both small ones, and he heaved them both to
the deck of the sailboat.

I had brought my own lunch along with me, and
the others had theirs too. I forget what theirs consisted
of, but I had included an orange in mine, one of the very
few still left from a small supply I had brought with me
from the *Nascopie.*

Bobby was familiar with oranges, and so were the
others. They had probably eaten a few, perhaps from the
mission when it was in operation, perhaps from the Post
store, or given to them by tourists when the ship was
in. I peeled the orange and could feel, rather than see,
all their eyes glued to my fingers as I worked at it. As
soon as I had finished, I glanced up, and all eyes turned

away in a flash. Without a word I handed it over to
Bobby.

"*Oovunga?*" he asked. "For me?"

"*Ee,*" I answered, and made a circular motion with my
hand to include everybody.

Carefully Bobby separated the sections of the orange
and handed them out, one by one, giving me my fair
share. They ate their pieces slowly, getting the last
morsel of taste out of each and licking the drops that
trickled down their fingers before they wandered an inch.
At last it was all gone, and then they noticed that I still
had my section. This I gave to Jimmy in spite of their
half-hearted protests that I should have it myself. They
all watched him as he grinned and chewed away at it,
having their pleasure all over again. It was a highly successful orange.

Late in the afternoon we sailed back to camp. There
were the two seals to be cut up, dogs to feed, notes to
write up, diary to enter, and all the little jobs of a field
camp. Bobby came in to have his thumb dressed once
more. The bandage had come off, just as I knew it would.
He had lost it that afternoon when he had to get a harpoon into one of those seals quickly before it sank and he
had had no time to think about bandages and sore thumbs.
However, it looked a lot better and the nail seemed determined to stay in place after all.

While I was playing surgeon to Bobby, loud wails from
little Jimmy made themselves heard. He fell down often
enough when he was running about, occasionally with
disastrous results, for so much of the landscape was solid
rock that a fall almost anywhere was apt to be painful.
He was no cry baby and never howled unless he was
really hurt; now, after a few loud wails, he stopped and
I paid no further attention to the matter. It was only
later that I learned that he had cut the palm of his left

hand quite deeply with an ulu. I offered to dress it, but
Jenny told me she had bound it up with a piece of cloth
and that he was asleep.

I saw the cut the next morning, long and fairly deep,
severing some of the upper muscle bundles, so I then had
two patients in my clinic. Jimmy was a bit scared of this
new medicine man at first, but Jenny assured him that he
wouldn't be hurt and calmed his fears. There was no
sense in putting a bandage anywhere on that restless
young mortal, so I merely cleaned the wound and held
the edges together with adhesive strips.

That morning we started work on the lower of the two
houses I had selected to be dug. There were two reasons
for this decision. The first was that by alternating
between the two houses we could give the frozen soil
time to thaw. The second, and less urgent, was that
Lily had now discovered, what I already knew, that just
beneath the grass roots lay the logs of driftwood which
had once supported the roof of sods and stones, still in
the position into which they had fallen when it collapsed,
and, in many cases, good sound wood though wet. Some
logs, lying in the wettest places, were as soft and mushy
as rain-soaked blotting-paper.

Lily had spotted these logs, when she wandered over
to see what we were up to, during one of her leisurely
prowls in search of firewood. She scented her prey, and
with the help of little Jimmy, entered with great enthusiasm on the task of assisting us to roll back the carpet of
green turf and grass.

I had got Bobby to understand that I wanted all the
logs left lying in place so that I could see how they had
been arranged and get a photograph of them, but when
Lily and Jimmy, quite uninstructed and in her case at
least with strong predatory instincts concerning wood,
added their efforts, I had more than I could manage.

Bobby saw the trouble and chased his wife and son off to their own tent, but it was with a good deal of difficulty that we convinced Lily that she might not take one of those fine big logs with her. I assured her that she would get all of them for her own as soon as possible and that we would stack them up in an openwork pile to dry in the sun and wind, but she grumbled at the delay, half convinced that it was mere spite which made me deny her a miserable stick of wood when there were dozens lying about, actually in my way!

Laying bare the roof of the old house was a good day's work, but we managed to get all the grass, roof-soil and stones out, and the logs exposed before knocking off for the day. Next morning, if the light should be good, I would photograph them and then we should be ready for the actual excavation.

Seal liver and bacon for dinner again, fried as usual. The Eskimos cook most of their food by boiling, for frying, roasting and baking are not practicable with native equipment and they have not yet all added these methods to their traditional cuisine, except in the case of those who live most of the time at or near the Post. Bannocks are fried or baked, but that's white man's food.

Bannock is a good Gaelic word meaning a cake, and not Eskimo as a gullible Frenchman assumed. He wrote it *banik*, unaware that there are no Eskimo words in the dialect of the eastern Arctic beginning with the letter *b*, except those founded on the recently introduced roots *baptism* and *beer*.

A bannock is a simple thing to cook and sticks to one's ribs amazingly well. That's what makes it so popular in the outlying parts of the world. Here's a recipe which you may find useful on a camping trip some time.

Open the top of your flour sack wide and scoop out a pit in the flour, about the size of your fist or a little larger. Into this pit pour a cup of cold water, stirring round and round as you do so with your left hand. The water will remain in the pit, wetting only the flour it actually touches. When the water is stirred in, add a heaping teaspoon of baking powder and a little salt.

Keep on stirring and the water will pick up more and more flour till you have a thin dough. The stirring may be done with a spoon, but the hand is better. When the dough is thick enough to lift out as a single soft ball, transfer it to a well-greased frying-pan. Here the ball of dough will collapse into a disk and spread out to make a bannock six or seven inches across and an inch or so thick. Hold the frying-pan over a fairly hot camp fire. When the underside of the bannock is brown, flip it up in the air, and catch it upside down in the pan, then brown the second surface. Keep the bannock on the move in the pan, or it may stick. Serve while hot; a cold bannock can be pretty heavy.

Everybody seemed anxious to get to work on the new igloo. It already looked a good deal more promising than the one we had started on first; it was bigger and we had not yet encountered the annoying frozen soil which slows operations so badly. Bobby and Mark wanted to get going with shovels and throw everything out but, as I was anxious not to miss any sign of stratification in the contents, we had to go at a somewhat slower pace than that.

I'm not much of a diplomat, but I knew that I had to get rid of my "helpers" for a time without hurting their feelings, so that I could look after things myself. After a few minutes' digging I stood up to straighten my back, which was something we all did at fairly regular intervals. This time, after the usual casual glance round the landscape, I stood "frozen," fixed and immobile, as

though I had seen something interesting. Soon Bobby
noticed my preoccupation and asked me what I saw.

"*Ahchook*," I answered. "*Chico, imaha.*" By which
I meant, "I'm not sure. Maybe it's just ice."

Now Bobby gathered that I had seen some white
object floating or, as he hoped, swimming in the water and
it might be a bear.

"*Nanook?*" he queried excitedly.

"*Imaha.*"

That last "Maybe" was enough for Bobby. In a
moment he and Mark were bounding down the slope to
their tent. They snatched up their rifles and some
ammunition and fled across the rocks to the boat. In
less than five minutes the sail was hoisted and they were
under way, in hot pursuit of some object which, as I had
distinctly said, I thought was merely a piece of floating
ice. They didn't really need much in the way of an
excuse anyhow; hunting is better than digging any day.

Soon Jenny joined me, working slowly and methodically
with a trowel, throwing nothing out without first examining it, even if it were just an ordinary stone. Together
we cleared one end of the igloo down to the level of a
sleeping platform on which a smooth floor of flag stones
had been laid.

It was becoming evident that this was a much more
carefully built igloo than the one on which we had first
started work. The general layout was becoming apparent
and one could see sleeping platforms, places for lamps,
a place where the meat was kept, and also a fine permanent
stone table conveniently placed for use when cooking.
Under the front edges of the sleeping platforms were
little nooks and crannies, intentionally arranged as convenient places in which to keep small treasures and
trinkets, as well as those tools, such as knives and whetstones, which were in frequent use.

Two pieces of ironware turned up lying on this sleeping platform and other signs of contact with white men were soon added to the specimen list. These, however, were few in comparison with the total number collected.

Towards evening Bobby and Mark returned. They had seen no bear, and had shot no seals, but that didn't matter because we had enough fresh meat on hand anyway, and seals were plentiful as a rule so there was no immediate danger of running out of it.

Bobby and Jimmy presented themselves in the evening to have their hands dressed. Both were making good progress and showed no signs of infection, which never failed to amaze me when I saw the incredible amount of dirt they managed to get into a wound. Jimmy was becoming quite fond of being attended to and watched everything with great interest.

Towards night the wind veered round to the north and got stronger, bringing much cooler weather with it. I had to tighten up the guy ropes on my tents and, in one or two places, fasten them to larger boulders. There is no thought of using tent pegs here, except in a few places to hold the bottom of the tent wall down. The tent itself is supported on poles which have to be brought in from the outside along with the tent rather than cut on the spot, for there isn't a stick of timber big enough for a tent pole within many miles. The guy ropes are stretched out to large stones, each weighing fifty pounds or more, and even then the continuous tugging of the ropes will drag these enough to loosen the tent. Bobby and Mark, seeing what I was doing, came over to help.

Bobby looked up at the sky, glanced about him with a weather-wise eye, and predicted rain.

Rapidly the wind grew stronger and, after I had gone to bed, I began to wonder if my small silk tent would stand through the night. A silk tent is not a good tent to sleep in, for the thin, stiffish material (which is not silk) is incredibly noisy and can imitate a wide range of sounds with disconcerting accuracy.

That night, as I lay half-way between sleep and waking, I could hear feet squelching in the soggy mosses outside my tent, bears snuffling at the doorway, the creak of oars in rowlocks and, most clearly of all, Bobby scrambling aboard his sailboat, heaving the anchor inboard and setting sail, though, as I ruminated drowsily, God knew I had given him no cause for deserting me on a barren island. All this I heard, and more, in the medley of noises made by that wretched little tent.

Then, towards morning, just as Bobby had said it would, the rain came and it drizzled and dripped all day long. I sat in my work tent, writing notes, cleaning specimens, numbering and packing them till I had caught up with all the things that had to be done. It was cold, clammy and damp in there, so, later in the day, I lit the Coleman stove to dry things out a bit. In just a few minutes I was warm and comfortable again and the whole world took on a more cheerful aspect.

My two patients came in for their daily dressing and stayed to talk. Jenny came in to see what I wanted to eat, and stayed to talk. Lily and Mark came to see where all the others had got to, and they, too, stayed to talk. It was a big crowd for so small a tent and all seats were taken.

We talked about many things, but I was a total loss as a conversationalist. We regretted the weather and hoped for improvement. We discussed the possibility of there being other house ruins on adjacent islands, but Bobby said he had never seen any except those where we were and the others which we had visited on MacColl Island.

We wondered about graves. We agreed that the houses

we were now working on were not very old, and were
certainly never occupied by the Tunnits. And we discussed the Tunnits.

Bobby had quite a lot to say about these mysterious
people, but I couldn't understand more than a bit of it and
I wouldn't have understood even that much if I had not
already read accounts of them.

Some people, and by people I mean Eskimo people,
say that the Tunnits were dwarfs, while others insist that
they were giants. Those who adhere to the dwarf
hypothesis insist that these little people still live in the
hills where they hunt lemmings with miniature bows and
arrows just as real people hunt caribou. They make their
clothes of lemming skins and live in crevices deep down in
the rocks where they are safe, not only from human
beings, but from the owls and foxes, the ravens and hawks
which pursue them unmercifully.

There is not much chance of any of the giants being
left though. The present Eskimo say that there were still
some when they first came into their present hunting-
grounds and that these giants used to capture the Eskimo
women and force them to marry them. The last of the
giants was killed by an Eskimo woman, thus forced into
a hateful marriage, who pierced his forehead with a bow-
drill while he slept. It must have been a singularly pro-
found slumber.

Bobby admitted that he had never seen either a giant
or a dwarf, but he was fully aware that other people, not
his own ancestors, had inhabited the country before they
had. He knew that stone implements of various kinds,
such as knives, scrapers and arrow points, which were to
be found lying about in various places, were made by
these strangers, for they were chipped from a kind of
stone, quartzite, which his own people never made use
of and of the very source of which they were ignorant.

There were none of these strange implements to be seen about our present camping-place, he assured me, but many of them could be found near his winter home, south of Purt Burwell.

By now my conversational powers were almost exhausted. I racked my brains for a topic that would employ at least some of the few words in my vocabulary. Surely there was something we could talk about! There were, of course, hundreds of things that I wanted to ask about—and couldn't. Bobby, all of them, wanted to ask me all about my life "outside," but they knew well enough that I couldn't understand their question and that I couldn't answer them even if they did make me understand.

I wondered then, and have often wondered since, whether our inability to exchange thoughts freely may not have had its advantages as well as its all too evident drawbacks. What if an ability to understand each other fully had led to that familiarity which breeds contempt!

If I could have found out most of the things about their habits which made them strange to me, in just a few days, might I not have found them less strange and less interesting?

If they had been able to penetrate the veil of mystery which my enforced silence threw about me, simply by asking me what they wanted to know and getting a direct answer, might they not have found me a good deal less mysterious?

If they once knew how little I knew about them and their way of life and their country, might they not have felt for me the amused and pitying contempt the city dweller feels for the rustic who is visiting the big town for the first time?

Finding nothing more to talk about, I brought out the loop of string which I used for making cat's cradles.

Jenny's eyes lit up at once and she took it with enthusiasm. I imagine she must have been more or less a local expert at making these intricate figures; certainly she seemed to have a larger repertoire than Tola had had, and she worked with more speed and assurance too.

I had with me a booklet showing diagrams of some figures collected in the western Arctic and Jenny examined these with great interest. Some she recognized at once and called them by name, though not always by the same name as was in the book. Others, which were not familiar to her, she would study for a minute or two and then, perhaps not at the first trial, she would produce the same result as shown in the book.

It was impossible to follow her speeding fingers, even when I asked her to slow down, but I am reasonably sure that she obtained her figures, in at least some cases, by steps other than those detailed as being used in the western Arctic.

She appeared to have a thorough comprehension of the basic principles by which the figures were governed. There are definite types of moves, such as shifting the top loop off certain fingers, or taking off an underlying loop, or changing the position of one or more loops to another finger or to the other hand. Each of these operations has a definite effect, modified by circumstances, and she knew what to anticipate as the result of each standard move. Her insight into the fundamentals of the whole complex gave her a facility in manipulating the strings which was denied to one not familiar with this pastime since childhood.

Quite definitely this booklet was one of the most interesting pieces of literature that had ever drifted into Jenny's ken. She thumbed it over again and again, ignoring questions and interruptions, forgetting even her cup of hot tea.

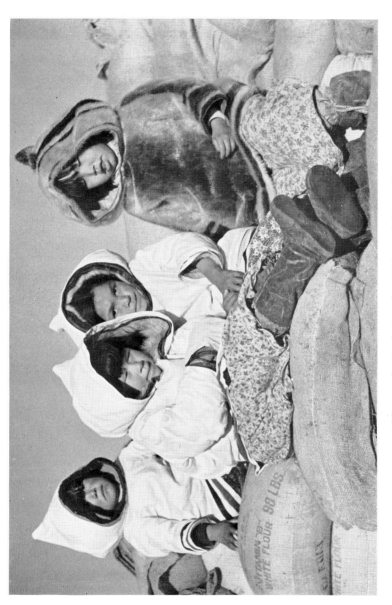

" No regular bed-time for Eskimo children "

" Unaccustomed to petting and none too trustful of any man "

"*Igvit?*" I enquired casually. "Do you want it?"

"*Oovunga?*"

"*Ee. Igvit.*"

Jenny looked at me. For a few moment she didn't speak, but just stared. Can he be fooling me? Could he possibly mean it's for me? Surely he can't. He must be saying this in mistake for something else!

One after another the thought shadows flitted across her face. Never have I seen anybody so elated, so utterly pleased.

"*Oovunga!*" she repeated, almost under her breath, and the tears sprang to the corners of her eyes.

I have a thousand books in my own library I suppose, and hundreds of thousands at my disposal should I need them. I had never realized before just how much one single book could mean.

Jenny is a girl of considerable intelligence, and her first action after getting the book was that of a scholar and a scientist. She seized at once on the fact that I had given her the names of some of the figures in the book, but she could not read the script in which these names were written. Would I please tell her again, so that she might note them down in syllabic?

It was a strain on my linguistic faculties, but between us we made it, in some cases at any rate. A few were easy enough, such as *tuktu*, the caribou, *tulugak*, the raven, and *netchek*, the seal, but when it came to such things as "two men carrying water buckets" (and they do seem to move along with the buckets bobbing about as the two men walk), it was just too much for my powers of translation.

Many of the figures, the more complex ones especially, are not static. They actually work. One favourite shows two men sitting in an igloo when suddenly a bear starts tearing down the walls, whereupon the two men most

I

wisely take refuge down a hole in the floor. The men are represented by two loops of string, sitting quietly enough, in a larger loop which is their house.

The performer now gives vent to horrifying growls. The two little men stir uneasily and then, not too hastily but with praiseworthy decision and a full realization of the wisdom of their course, shrink until they have finally vanished completely under the floor of their igloo. The destructive bear is never visible, being represented only by off-stage noises, but no Eskimo infant watching the show ever has any doubts at all as to the actuality and immediate presence of that house-rending bear!

Taking it all round, there's nothing like a session with string figures to make one's guests feel at home.

Chapter X

JENNY'S COOKING

W E had been on the Button Islands just about a week when Bobby reminded me that the next day was Sunday. We had crossed Gray Straits on a Sunday and that was at his own choice, for he had been just as tired of waiting for clear weather as I had, but now things were different and he felt that we should observe the day as one of rest.

I think most Eskimos would agree that one of the brightest ideas ever to occur to a white man was to knock off work one day in seven. The fact that this taboo didn't originate in our culture at all but far away and long ago makes no difference. It's a fine idea and no Eskimo who has once felt its advantages is going to relinquish his right to a weekly holiday. Bobby was not, as far as I could determine, arguing from moral or religious principles; the exegetical aspect of the matter was far beyond him, as it is far beyond most of us, but a holiday is a holiday whether it is also a holy day or not.

It is a day for peaceful strolls through one's own private grounds and that's just how we celebrated it. In spite of the continuing bad weather we made a tour of the island, finding an old grave with two skulls in it and a *kayak* and a *komatik* (sled) near by. These had once been placed on the graves but had been dislodged, either by bears or by the wind.

It's astonishing what the violent winter gales can do.

There is no shrubbery, of course, to arrest the force of the wind, no trees to provide shelter, and the gales blow over the naked rocks, even in summer, with great violence.

We climbed to the summit of the highest peak on Lacy Island and, near the top, I found a sizeable stick of wood resting among the rocks. It was perhaps six feet long and about three inches thick, just about right for a harpoon shaft, and Bobby promptly commandeered it for exactly that purpose.

"How did it get up here?" I enquired.

"*Anore!*" explained Bobby. "The wind."

Now, a wind strong enough to carry a stick of that size eight hundred feet uphill is no gentle summer breeze.

Some weeks later, Jenny and I were walking about the country some half-mile from her winter home and found a blue, knitted, woollen cap lying on the ground, bleached almost white on the side that was exposed to the weather. Two or three years before it had adorned the infant head of little Jimmy, had been blown off in a strong wind and carried away. Possibly the dogs had found it and had carried it even farther than the wind had, but that was not likely for the dogs would have gulped down anything that smelt so strongly of the human body as that.

Eskimo dogs are firmly convinced that anything that smells good *is* good. Good to eat, they mean. This includes a great variety of things which, in our opinion, smell bad and are decidedly *not* good to eat. First of all, anything of animal origin, which includes all mammals, birds, fish, everything in fact except plants and minerals, is definitely good, whether fresh or rotten, wet or dry, living or killed, found or stolen.

Rotten meat, so putrid that no unaccustomed white man can stand to leeward of it for a moment, is obviously good choice food and the dogs bolt it with gusto, rolling in ecstasy where it lay, thereby soaking their coats with its most desirable perfume. The gentlemen who write the advertisements for scents would find new inspiration could they but meet with a husky, as the Eskimo dogs are often called, fresh from these delirious exercises.

Occasionally the dogs are lucky enough to find a dead walrus or seal on the beach before their masters discover it. They eat their way into the soft belly, work themselves into the carcass, and there they feed at their leisure in a fleshy Aladdin's cave of fine meat and perfumed air.

After exhausting the meats, next in order of desirability, according to the dogs, is the excreta of animals, both human and non-human. Leaving camp in the morning for a stroll, as nature demands that one must, is a signal for the dogs to arise and follow. A good stout stick is a necessary possession at that moment, to ward off the more eager, or one may find oneself in a wild mêlée of contesting dogs, who have no interest in the man and care not in the least what befalls him. Even should one succeed in leaving camp unobserved, the keen noses of the dogs will bring them to the scene in a very few minutes, and from quite incredible distances.

Third in degree of desirability, and still high in the scale, is anything that smells as if it *might* be good to eat. This includes such things as discarded bits of sealskin shoes, old bits of skin clothing, short ends of rope that have been much handled, pieces of wood that have been grasped continuously such as whip handles and so taste and smell of human hands, or even stones that have been lying in close contact with something edible, such as those on which a carcass once rotted.

Bits of cloth are a menace to Eskimo dogs, for they will be bolted in a second if they smell strongly of human body odours but, unlike the skin clothing, they are quite indigestible, will block the dog's intestines and, quite possibly, kill him. Bits of rope are not quite so bad, for

the dog chews them into small pieces which unravel while
being passed through the intestines and the animal is able
to void the remnants in most cases. The stones which a
dog may lick and slobber over, he will seldom actually
swallow, so they are less of a menace.

So little Jimmy's cap, blown from his head by the gale
of two or three years ago, was probably never swallowed
by a dog, but was carried half a mile at least by the wind.

We had a fine view of Lacy Island from the top of
the hill. We got a new impression and a better comprehension of the other islands of the group, all of which
lay to the south-west of us. We could see the open water
of Hudson Strait to the north, east and west, and far off
due north was a dim object which we took to be Resolution
Island, "if it isn't merely fog!" as Bobby commented.

On our way down again we came across the tracks
of a small polar bear, but they were not very fresh.
Nowhere did we see any hares, or foxes, or ptarmigan.
In many sheltered spots, in deep gullies, and in the lee of
some of the cliffs, there was snow still lying in dirty
drifts, dripping its life away in the warmer weather of
summer. Some of these drifts would never go, said
Bobby, for fresh snow would cover them again before
they could finish melting. If, in the course of centuries,
the weather as a whole gets colder, the snowdrifts which
fail to melt in summer will become larger and more
numerous and, if the cold continues, will increase till once
again the northern part of the continent is sheathed in
thick ice as it was thousands of years ago.

Jenny appeared in my tent that evening with a carelessly crumpled dish towel in her hands. When we first
set up house-keeping together I had presented her with
two new dish towels, explaining that one was for her use
and the other for mine. I was still a good deal too
fastidious in those days! My idea was to see to it that my

dishes would not be wiped with the same towel that served for their dishes. Both dish towels were identical and, therefore, indistinguishable, and—what did it matter anyway?

Under the dish towel which she carried was a plate of seal liver and fried potatoes, a favourite dish. She laid this down on the table and then, with all the nonchalance of a modest but highly competent magician, she produced some tea biscuits from the innocent-looking dish towel.

She was immensely flattered by my expressions of delight and amazement. Sincere enough, too, for I had no idea that she was going to make tea biscuits or that she could, for that matter. Of course, I had to try one of them, then and there.

Not so good! Quite definitely not so good, but I went ahead and devoured it as quickly as a husky dog would have done rather than let her down.

Tea biscuits appeared fairly often on the menu after that, and they were always produced from the dish towel as an afterthought with an air of careless ease. We were both mighty proud of them—she, because she could make them, and I, because I could eat them.

Little Jimmy was now becoming quite accustomed to the *kablunah* and would invite me to share in his games. He would come to me, too, when he was hurt or wanted something done for him. His needs were few and simple, though, and he played quite happily by himself or with Sammy, the "white" dog.

Jimmy was blessed with a large and conspicuous Mongolian spot. This is a patch of bluish pigmentation in the skin at the lower part of his back right above the buttocks. It is very common among Eskimo children, though not perhaps universal, and the mothers are very proud of it, saying that it is the mark of the true Eskimo. Actually it is shared by nearly all people of Mongolian origin, including the Chinese and Japanese, the Mongols, the Indians of both North and South America, some of the natives of India, and various people in Europe including some Prussians and Hungarians whose ancestry holds remnants of the invading Mongol hordes.

I had noticed two little children at the outer sealing camp where we had waited to make our crossing, both of whom showed good Mongolian spots. One, a little boy, had two spots, one just at the upper end of the division between the buttocks and a second spot about two inches above it; each spot was a couple of inches across. The other, a girl, had perhaps five spots irregularly distributed just above the sacrum.

The largest Mongolian spot I ever saw was on a little girl named Lena who lived at Pangnirtung in Baffin Island. The doctor at the hospital there called my attention to it and I tried to get a photograph, but with poor results as the blue of the spot was merely white or normal skin colour in the photograph. This spot extended from the top of the buttocks right up the back to the left shoulder blade and armpit.

These spots usually vanish as the child grows up and by the age of five or six they have completely disappeared, though there are exceptional cases in which they persist into later years.

Jimmy, though he was now four, still nursed at his mother's breasts. Often he would stop in his play and run over to her, nurse for a few minutes, and then run outside again. Eskimo children are often suckled till they are a good deal older than he was and there are tales of children who alternated between the breast and a cigarette.

Jimmy, I regret to report further, dribbled. He dribbled perpetually and continuously, so that the bib of the overalls which he usually wore was always soaking wet. He made no effort to wipe away the swinging, ropy drool. He appeared quite unconscious of it and neither Jenny nor Lily paid any attention to it either.

Mark dribbled too, and he must have been twenty if he was a day. Less than Jimmy did, by a good deal, but he, too, made no effort to do anything about it. Especially when he laughed, and he was nearly always laughing, he dribbled. It was almost a sign of his good humour.

Now that we were settled down in camp Jenny developed an experimental mood in cooking. Perhaps the memories of the days when she had cooked for white men before were returning to her. One morning, rummaging through my possessions, she came across some rolled oats and immediately she showed signs of delighted recognition. She bore off the package to her tent and, at breakfast the next morning, served up the porridge. It was good too, except for the fact that there were tea leaves in it. Quite a lot of tea leaves, in fact.

Jenny was well aware that this was not the way Mrs. Beeton would have done things, and mentioned the fact that she had only one pot to cook with and that she had made tea in it just before. This I took as both an explanation and a promise that it wouldn't happen again.

I was still in the stage of being a little fussy about my food, still am for that matter, so I picked out the tea leaves and discarded them.

Next morning, more porridge and more tea leaves. This time, after picking them out, I ranged them round the edge of my plate in a more or less decorative border and they were still there when Jenny came to get the plates to wash up. I didn't mean to hurt her feelings, but just to let her know that I didn't propose to eat them. I knew she would solve the problem after that little hint.

She did. Never again did she produce porridge and never again did either of us mention the word.

Meanwhile, work on the "Lower North" igloo, the second of the two to be opened, was continuing with quite interesting results. It was an extensive building, large enough for fifteen or more people to sleep in without overcrowding. The sleeping platforms were wide and large and formed of carefully laid stones. It must have been used for a number of years, for the construction was far too careful for a mere temporary hut.

At lunch-time one day, Lily came in to have her finger dressed. She had cut the top off some time ago and now she complained of pain down her finger and into her wrist. I washed it out as well as possible and saw no signs of suppuration. I put a dressing on it and decided to do no more unless it grew worse. That made three of my family of five decorated with adhesive tape.

Jimmy still came regularly to have his dressing changed. He would flatten out his palm and spread his fingers wide so that I could get at the cut, stretching the skin of his palm so much that the healed edges would spring open again. This would amuse him greatly and he would peer at the red muscle beneath the skin and laugh aloud. However, it was beginning to heal from the bottom and there were still no signs of infection.

Bobby and Mark spent practically the whole of that day in seal hunting, but with no success. They did succeed in shooting a seagull and Jenny promptly put it to use by sweeping out the floor cloths of my two tents with one of its wings. A bird's wing makes a good hand whisk and is used a great deal by the Eskimos.

Jenny is a most energetic person. She worked hard on the igloo all day, slowly and carefully, did some laundry for me, and cooked my meals as well.

Lily was definitely not so clean in her person as were

the others. When she stood close to me while I was dressing her finger it was quite apparent that she smelt bad. None of the others had any particular odour about them as far as I could tell, except that there was an unpleasant "little boy" smell about Jimmy, probably because the sour saliva of his dribbling soaked the front of his clothes.

There were no signs of lice on any of them, nor did I notice any on any of the other Eskimos I met. That is not to say that no Eskimos have lice, however!

Specimens were increasing in number by now and I had over a hundred from the larger igloo. There were pieces of bone, ivory and antler, which showed the marks of tools, bird bones used to make an ornamental fringe on a dress, whetstones, scrapers, the figure of a bear carved in a soft red stone, combs made from caribou antler, and so on.

Later that evening Jenny came to my tent to show me that she had solved the problem of one of the string figures in the book. She had been puzzling over it for a long time and was unable to do it a day or two before, but now she had it right. I was not at all sure that she did it by the method described however.

Reading matter is always a problem on field trips to distant regions. One takes along some solid books that will last long and well repay reading. Each man to his own taste, of course, but for me it's always a difficult problem and the fact that I've had to make the choice fairly often has not made it any easier. Sometimes circumstances have permitted but one book; on others, as on this occasion, several could be carried easily enough.

I prefer, for field work, a book that will permit frequent interruption, a book that can be picked up and opened almost at random. The three books which I had selected for this trip were Bates' *Naturalist on the Amazon*, Dar-

win's *Origin of Species*, and Lawrence's *Letters*. That's
D.H., not T.E.

My progress in speaking Eskimo, though slow, was
undoubted. I had accumulated a vocabulary of sorts and
had now got to the stage where I was digesting what I had
already acquired, resting on one of the plateaux of learning of which the pedagogues tell us. Now I took a step
forward, more or less by force, for there was something
that I wanted to tell Bobby about, and it had to be done
in his language.

We were pausing for a smoke after an hour's work on
the igloo. I turned deliberately to address Bobby, for I
wanted his full attention. It is useless to try to reproduce
my broken Eskimo, but the gist of my story was
this:

"Bobby! Last night I was asleep in my tent. I heard
a growl. I though it must be a bear. I sat up and
listened. There it was again. And again. I got out of
bed. I grasped my rifle. I went to the door of my tent.
I heard the noise again. There was no bear. It was only
Bobby snoring!"

My effort was entirely successful, for I was understood,
fully and at once. Bobby and Mark and Jenny went off
into peals of laughter. Lily came running out of the tent
to find out what it was all about and the story had to be
told again, with pantomime, for her benefit. Then she
howled too!

After we had all subsided a bit, we went back to work,
but for the rest of that day, and for days to come, whenever an unusual silence occurred, somebody would snore
and we would laugh all over again.

One evening, when things were dragging a bit, Jenny
and Bobby were sitting in my tent chatting and smoking. I dug down into the recesses of one of my supply
boxes while they looked on with interest. There was

never any knowing what might be produced from those boxes.

This time it was a cardboard box of simple jig-saw puzzles.

Jenny hailed them with delight, for she had met them before, she told me. Promptly she and Bobby got to work, one puzzle each. In both cases the completed picture would be of things unfamiliar to Eskimos, but this was no bar and they worked steadily ahead with as much well-directed effort as an intelligent white man would muster.

Jenny was quicker than Bobby by a little, even though his picture was fairly easy, representing as it did a man fishing for trout in a mountain stream, a scene of which at least some of the elements were recognizable. Jenny, on the other hand, had some picture or other that meant but little to her.

When the two pictures were complete, Jenny handed them back to me, but I urged her to keep them, explaining that she could give them to little Jimmy to play with.

She snorted indignantly. "Shimmy!" she said, in a tone which implied clearly enough that Jimmy would be a good deal older before he was allowed to play with such treasures.

Bobby sat back from his task and looked at me with an expectant grin.

"What else have you got?" asked Jenny, clearly enough and intent of making a night of it.

Once more I plunged into my store box and brought out a ridiculous little toy I had had made for me before leaving. I had already tried it on the sedate scientists of the Geological Survey of Canada and found it good.

It consisted of a wooden tube at one end of which was a shorter upright tube. Blowing through it produced a little fountain of air. When a light ball of cork was placed on this jet, it would dance and balance on it, just as the celluloid balls do on the water jets in a shooting gallery.

Piercing the cork ball was a wire, one end of which ended in a hook. Thrust into the horizontal wooden tube, just ahead of the upright vent, was another wire, also hooked.

Now, blowing gently through the tube would make the cork ball dance, and the aim of the performer was so to regulate his blowing as to lift the cork ball neatly and gently, hooking its wire on to the standing hook. It required care and skill, but would not be too difficult a task, except for one fact.

The tube is short and, to watch the progress of events one must necessarily cross one's eyes. Then one's face soon acquires a rich, red tinge from the breathing exercises, and one is further handicapped by the effort required to avoid breaking into howls of maniacal laughter.

Everybody else is laughing, the cork wavers and hovers, turning and twisting like a dancing marionette and evading with diabolical skill the patient hook which stands waiting to receive it. It's a highly amusing toy.

Once more our howls of mirth brought the others running out of their tent to see what on earth we were up to now.

No sooner did we hear the thudding of their soft-shod feet than we thrust the toy away under something or other and sat, serious and sober, when inquisitive heads were poked in at the door.

"What?" demanded Mark.

"Nothing!" we all assured him.

I don't remember the Eskimo expression for "Like fun!" or "Oh, yeah?" but Mark made use of it then and sat himself down, clearly determined to stay till he found out what it was all about.

With a straight and sober face, I handed him the little pipe and explained what had to be done.

Mark took it in his hand, crossed his eyes, and started to blow. His first puff shot the cork to the roof of the tent. Bobby and Jenny howled, little Jimmy fell over in his efforts to retrieve it, and the two black husky pups outside started to howl.

Mark tried again—and again—and once more. He swore his blankets would never see him again till he had succeeded. We adjourned well after midnight, with a score of three to his credit.

" And I bet my eyes stay crossed for ever! " he said, as they wished me a good sleep, and took the little trail down to their own tent.

Chapter XI

THE CONJUROR'S PLATFORM

TAKING it all round, we had rotten weather. My diary is peppered with comments on the continuous high winds, the perpetual rain, the grey depressing scuds of cloud. Nor is this anything new for Killinek Island and its vicinity. In 1884, when H. M. Burwell was the officer in charge of the meteorological station he recorded a "tremendous gale" on the 24th of November. At 5.15 in the afternoon it registered 84 miles per hour, and then the cups were blown clean off the anemometer. It was quite a relief when a fine day did come along, as they actually did on occasion, but the Eskimos took it all as a matter of everyday routine, which it was to them.

In spite of everything, we had made a good deal of progress on the lower north igloo, which was now quite clearly revealed and all its interior arrangements could be distinguished. Its greatest length was twenty-seven feet and its width fourteen. There were three sleeping platforms, each standing about eighteen inches above the general floor level. One of them occupied a sort of alcove at the west end of the building, the other two were end to end along the north wall, separated from each other by only a slight difference in elevation.

There was a special place where the lamp had stood, just inside the door, to the right. Here the ground was soaked with seal oil and grease, the volatile elements of which had all evaporated, leaving a thick tar-like sub-

" A bannock is a simple thing to cook "

" A much more carefully built igloo "

stance which cemented the underlying sand and gravel into a material resembling asphalt. In this, too, were occasional specimens. Just behind the lamp was a bench on which the meat had been kept, and a second meat-bench stood just to the left of the entrance.

In the north-west corner, between two of the sleeping platforms, a flat slab of rock formed a table. All the interior structures of the igloo were thus explained and

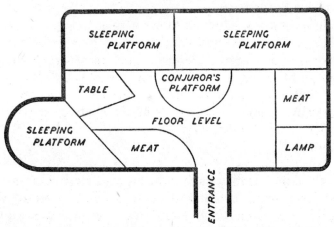

DIAGRAM OF THE INTERIOR OF THE LOWER NORTH IGLOO

accounted for with the exception of a podium-like arrangement of flat stone which projected into the middle of the floor, opposite the separation between the two north sleeping platforms.

"What was this for?" I asked Bobby.

His answer was a delighted grin. Without a word, he mounted the little stand and, twisting and contorting his body in imitation of the medicine men of pre-Christian days, he began a weird and haunting little song. It was the conjuror's platform.

He explained in more detail when we had an interpreter.

K

Here the medicine man, the *angokok*, would stand when he was repeating incantations to bring good weather, to ensure a catch of seals, to speed the recovery of a sick woman. Here, too, stood the drummer when the people sang and danced in the long winter nights.

Bobby had never seen any of these performances, but his father had told him of them and, he said, many of the older men could still remember them well. It is by no means certain that they are even yet extinct in some of the remoter settlements.

In most cases, large flat stones with at least one straight edge had been selected to form the front rows of paving flags for the sleeping platforms, and these were so large that they could be undermined in front sufficiently to permit the formation of small recesses under the edge. In these little hidey-holes we found numbers of specimens which the last inhabitants of the igloo had left behind them.

When that was, and why they left, we shall probably never know. It may be that the growing settlement in the neighbourhood of the mission at Killinek attracted the people and drew them away from the outlying winter camps, or it may be that the decline in whaling in the eastern Arctic resulted in a shift of population. In any case, it is evident that the igloo was still in use when white men had reached the country and their trade goods were fairly common, as the iron and pottery showed.

Eventually the roof had collapsed and made further use of the building impossible. This, fortunately, had happened when it was vacant for there were no human bones inside to indicate that anybody had been trapped by its fall.

It is easy to picture life as it must have been in those days. The main dependence of the people was on the meat they were able to obtain for themselves, and hunt-

ing was the daily occupation of the men. At night, when
they returned with their day's catch of seals, and the meat
had been cut up, the offal thrown to the dogs and the
edible portions brought into the igloo and laid safely on
the meat racks, the people sat upon the sleeping platforms,
listening to the hunters telling the tales of their experi-
ences.

Always they would dramatize the day's adventures.
They imitated the animals they had attacked and described in vivid pantomime their efforts to escape, with
a mimicry rendered perfect by years of observation of
the habits and movements of their prey.

Even the words that the pursued animal might be
expected to have spoken were repeated, and the women
and children listened enraptured. The women would
pause in their work of cutting up bits of meat for the soapstone pot, or shaping a piece of seal skin for a boot. The
little children would imitate all the gestures of the
hunters, growl when they growled, laugh with glee when
the hunter was successful and mourn with him when he
had to admit that the biggest one got away.

Then came the boiled seal-meat, and the rich hot
soup in which it had seethed so long. Having eaten to
repletion, the Eskimos would sit about the dimly lit igloo,
stripped to the waist to be more comfortable in the
stifling hot atmosphere, listening while one of the old
men told them tales of long ago, of how the world was
made, of how Sedna, the guardian spirit of the seals,
looked after her wards, and what men must do and must
not do to win her favour.

Theirs was a hard and dangerous life; to our minds
it was crude, primitive, uncouth. But it was a happy
life. There were no traders to demand fox skins, there
were no missionaries to say "Don't!", there were a few
whalers who willingly gave the men rare treasures for a

little work, and the women almost anything they asked in return for a little play. The people were healthy, happy, wealthy and wise, according to their own standards. To-day they are not so happy, neither according to our standards, nor to theirs.

Jenny displayed another of her accomplishments one evening by making shadows on the tent wall. She used only her fingers and hands, but the pictures were surprisingly realistic, both in shape and in movement. One of her most successful was a rabbit, or rather an Arctic hare, which sat up on its haunches, wriggled its nose, scratched its cheek and waggled its ears with astonishing realism.

Bobby tried his hand at one of the jig-saw puzzles that evening and was most insistent that he be allowed to do it alone. He didn't want help from anybody. He was a little slower than Jenny had been in doing the same puzzle but stayed at it till it was completed.

He had been busy making a large float of seal skin for use with his harpoon. He took the skin off a fairly small seal, making as few incisions as possible, and even those few were as small as he could make them. Now he had the float blown up tight and hanging just inside the entrance to his tent where it would swing in the wind till dry.

Jenny had been hard at work too. She always was, for the matter of that, never seeming to have an idle moment. Perhaps that is hardly true, for never was anybody more willing to go for a walk, but even her walks she turned to good account, picking up bits of firewood whenever she came across them. Now and then she would pick up a bit of strongly coloured red stone, spit on it and rub it on a near-by boulder to find out whether it would make a good red paint or not. She had no particular use for red paint, but it is almost the only pigment these people are familiar with except charcoal, and it is apparently usual to test all red stones which look as though they might serve as a source of pigment. In some of the old houses one finds pebbles of haematite which are faceted from being ground down to provide paint.

Jenny's work in spare moments for the last day or two had been cutting out boots from a cured seal skin. I say cured advisedly for they use no tanning process in the chemical sense. When Jenny gets the skin from a seal, she scrapes the remnants of fat and other tissues from the inside and shaves the hair from the outside, unless the skin is to be used for some garment which will have the hair left on it.

Once the skin has been shaved and scraped down to its final thickness it is pegged out to dry. To accomplish this, a grassy spot is selected if possible, and exposed to direct sunlight. Slits are cut in the edge of the skin and through these wooden pegs are passed. The skin is held by the pegs, not in direct contact with the ground, but about three inches above it so that the wind can get at both sides to speed the drying and also so as to keep it away from the grass and other vegetation which would almost certainly be wet. A grassy spot is chosen because it is here that the pegs find soil enough to hold in.

While the skins are drying, at the first sign of rain or mist they are taken off their pegs, rolled up and brought inside. As soon as it clears up they go out again, only to disappear once more, like Monday's washing, if the rain starts to fall.

Cutting out the pattern for boots is not a very difficult process, for the pattern is a simple one; however, the sewing of a watertight seam is one of the most painstaking of jobs and requires years of practice. When a girl can sew a good pair of boots her education is complete! The really intricate patterns are those used for making the heavy winter clothing of caribou skins, though the actual

sewing is much easier than for boots. Here the most
complex designs are used, both to shape the garment and
to secure the decorative effects which they achieve by
using strips of fur of contrasting colours. From the
animal's belly they get strips of white, and brown from
the back. Black can be had by proper treatment of the
dehaired skin, and red by rubbing the shaved leather with
the red stones which give pigment.

All these complex patterns are carried in the woman's
head, and their use requires considerable powers of
visualization and a good sense of form. Even the minor
variations required by the different sizes and shapes of
individuals are allowed for mentally and the Eskimo
seamstress would be much ashamed if the garment she
made for a man turned out to be ill-fitting.

Jenny was busy on a pair of boot soles, using the sharp
corner of her *ulu* as a stylus for marking the pattern on
the leather. She had no template or anything of that sort,
and apparently employed only the technique of the
precocious child artist who said he just thought of the right
shape and then drew a line round it.

She cut out one small pair of soles, evidently for little
Jimmy and inscribed his name on them with her *ulu* in
the syllabic script these people have learnt from the missionaries. Next she cut out a larger pair and wrote two
signs on them, so the name of the prospective owner would
be one or two syllables.

"Par-pee," she said as she did so, for they use no letter
"b" and Bobby is pronounced almost Parpee.

Then she cut out a much larger pair and turned to me
with a great air of mystery.

"What does that mean?" she asked.

I pretended great bewilderment. I counted the three
syllables and smote my brow in perplexity.

"*Tingmiak?*" I suggested.

Now *tingmiak* means a bird, and I knew perfectly well that Jenny was not undertaking to supply the ravens with footgear.

"*Auka!*" she said emphatically. "No!" and roared with amusement at the idea.

"*Kablunah?*" I asked. She sighed with relief and grinned.

ā		e		o		u		FINALS	
	▽		△		▷		◁		
pā	V	*pe*	∧	*po*	>	*pu*	<	*p*	<
tā	U	*te*	∩	*to*	)	*tu*	(	*t*	⊂
kā	९	*ke*	ᕈ	*ko*	ᑯ	*ku*	ᑲ	*k*	ᑲ
gā	ᒉ	*ge*	ᒥ	*go*	J	*gu*	Ⴑ	*g*	Ⴑ
mā	ᒉ	*me*	Γ	*mo*	⌐	*mu*	L	*m*	L
nā	ᔾ	*ne*	σ	*no*	ᔪ	*nu*	ᕐ	*n*	ᕐ
sā	ᕚ	*se*	ᕼ	*so*	ᕀ	*su*	ᕗ	*s*	ᕗ
lā	ᔆ	*le*	ᑕ	*lo*	ᔆ	*lu*	ᑕ	*l*	ᑕ
yā	ᕪ	*ye*	ᕫ	*yo*	ᕬ	*yu*	ᕤ		
vā	Ⅴ	*ve*	⋀	*vo*	⋗	*vu*	⋖	*v*	⋖
rā	ᕝ	*re*	ᕞ	*ro*	?	*ru*	९	*r*	९

ESKIMO SCRIPT SYLLABLES

"*Ee. Kablunah.*" Sure enough, they were for me.

The syllabic script has proved a blessing indeed to the Eskimos. Before the coming of the missionaries, they knew no way of writing, but they soon saw the advantages of it and learned quickly, passing the knowledge on from one to the other with surprising rapidity and accuracy. To-day many, if not most, of the Eskimos in the eastern

Arctic can read it and they write to each other a good
deal. They have some books printed in syllabics, principally of a religious nature. Official government notices
are also printed in it and are perfectly well understood
by the people.

I don't know whether Bobby was getting tired of seal-
meat, or whether he was merely tired of work, but one
day he borrowed my field glasses and went out in the
hope of getting a polar bear. The sea was far too rough
for seals and I couldn't see that there was chance of his
finding a bear either.

When the Button Islands were surveyed in 1912 by
Captain F. Anderson (the islands bear the names of his
assistants, J. H. Knight, H. H. Lawson, A. M. Lacy and
E. B. MacColl), he reported that they saw many bears,
but we did not see nearly so many as I had expected.
Actually we had seen none so far, and the tracks of two
only.

Late in the afternoon Bobby returned with no bear
and, to conceal his disappointment, he took Mark out with
him again to have a few shots at the seagulls with the ·22
rifle. They could not have retrieved them even if they
had hit any, which they did not.

More rain, and I had to rescue some specimens which
had been laid out to dry, instead of which they got soaked
even more thoroughly than they had already been. We
still had strong winds at night and my tent did its
best to keep me awake with false cries of danger and
alarm.

SATURDAY, AUGUST 17. Good weather to-day and I
was able to finish excavating the upper layer of the
Lower North igloo, clear the passage, draw a plan of it
to scale and take several photographs. During the evening I found another grave on the side of the hill which
had not been disturbed and a nice cache of objects

beside it, including a very nice wooden bowl with the handle still complete, part of a bird dart, a bow and parts of a harpoon.

So reads a typical entry from my diary of those days. We worked whenever we could, often in spite of bad weather, and after working we wandered about the island to see what we could find.

They were very delightful, those walks. There were so many things to see, so many to comment on, so many questions to ask. There were birds and flowers, berries and fungi, spiders and beetles, and an occasional butterfly.

It was a brave new world, filled with new things, new impressions, new wonderings. Most of them I had to keep to myself, for I still could express only the simplest thoughts in Eskimo, but it was surprising how well we did make ourselves understood.

There was, too, such an understanding between us, such a companionship as I have seldom felt with other people. My Eskimo family were always most considerate, most kindly, enquiring often as to my well-being and happiness. It was not that they considered me incompetent or a weakling, but rather that they realized or appeared to sense that this was not my normal way of life, just as this was not my normal environment. I may be deceived, but I like to think that they found me as congenial as I found them and that their kindliness was not a mere formality demanded by politeness, or a manifestation of that gratitude which is but "a lively sense of favours yet to come."

Jenny was sewing the sealskin boots she had cut out a day or so before when I sat down beside her on the sunny side of her tent. The waterproof seam she used is very ingenious and, if properly done, will never leak even though one stands in water for a long time. Actually it is a double seam and the stitches, though they catch in the leather, do not go through it. The sewing is done with fine threads of sinew from the caribou's back.

When a caribou is killed, the long strips or ribbons of sinew which lie on each side of the backbone are peeled off and, after washing and scraping, hung up to dry. They form a flat strip about four inches wide, an eighth of an inch thick, and two feet or more long.

When the sinew strips are dry, they can be teased out into very fine threads and these are used for sewing with, first moistening them either in the mouth or in a bowl of water to render them flexible. The sinew is very strong and will last much longer than would cotton thread. Moreover, when the sinew gets wet it swells up and tightly fills the perforation through which it passes.

Sometimes the sinew is braided into cords, about a sixteenth of an inch in diameter. This was extensively used in the olden days for anything that required both great strength and flexibility. Some of the braiding which was done in making harpoon lines for attaching the toggle to the main thong was very intricate and, though much less is made of it nowadays, most Eskimo women can braid very quickly and neatly using three, four or five threads with equal ease.

While I was watching Jenny sewing, Bobby had been making preparations to beach his boat on a smooth gravelly shore which shelved gradually. At high tide he sailed her gently aground and, when the tide had fallen, she tilted easily over on her side and let him get at the place on her bottom which was leaking.

I didn't see the details of his repair work, but it was apparently satisfactory, for she floated again when the tide returned and allowed him to take her back to her anchorage in the little cove, ferrying himself and Mark back and forth on the kayak, always a tricky performance, for it is a top-heavy kind of craft in any case and takes a bicycle rider's balance to manage. When a passenger rides stretched out at full length on the after deck, the centre of gravity is raised a foot or more and the kayak is even more inclined to tip than before.

During the afternoon, Bobby held the tape for me while I made a plan of the site, in spite of the fact that it was a Sunday. It's all very well to insist on your right not to work, but when there's nothing else to do, a little job of helping somebody else is sometimes a relief.

After I had got all the points I wanted included and a rough map made, Bobby wandered off to a long cascade of rocks which wandered down a gentle slope near the lower north igloo. Here and there among the stones he found a number of specimens and more beneath the turf. I think there must have been some old graves among the rocks even though we could see no bones, but Bobby insisted that an attack had been made on the people who had lived in the igloos and that they had lost some of their weapons here and had never recovered them, for the men had all been killed. He explained this at length when we had an interpreter, but I couldn't make out whether he was telling of something he knew to be fact or merely a tradition.

During the evening I re-drew my map with care, a process which greatly interested Bobby and Jenny. They were well able to read a map and understand at once the meaning of the symbols when explained to them. Many of them draw quite good maps themselves, but they are apt to be a bit shaky in matters of scale. This is partly psychological, for an unimportant or very simple part of a coast line will be drawn on a small scale and the next few miles, where there are important landmarks to look out for and dangers to be avoided, will be given as much space as the preceding fifty. Once this characteristic is understood and if the maker has explained it to the man who is to use it, an Eskimo map may prove even more valuable (though admittedly less accurate) than one drawn with all the resources and instruments of modern surveying.

When my map was finished, we were at a loss for amusement. We were tired of the jig-saw puzzles, I had not brought any cards with me, the "blow-up" toy took too much wind for daily use, and conversation was about exhausted. I still had paper and pencils on the table and decided to see if they knew the game of noughts and crosses.

It was quite new to them and I had to play both sides of the board, one for me and one for my opponent, for the first few games till they got the principles clear in their minds, but from then on it was anybody's game.

"*Pingashoot!*" Bobby would yell when he got three in a line, and jab his pencil down to make a cross in a vacant spot while, even before his victory was conceded, Jenny would be drawing the grid for the next game. I've still got some of them in a notebook somewhere. The paper isn't very clean, but it's full of memories.

Next morning we were all back at work on the igloo again, except Lily and Jimmy who were excused all excavation duties. We had finished work down to the most recent occupation level, all the flat stones making the platforms were revealed, and we were now going to take these up to see if there was another layer below.

Sure enough there was and under that yet another. There was about three inches of soil between the layers, and the lower pavements were less carefully laid than was the topmost one. Nothing in the intervening strata of soil revealed any secrets of the history of the building and I was not able to tell whether the different stone floor-

ings had been laid down by different families who re-
occupied the building after its abandonment by its original
builders, or whether a younger generation had decided
that the old home needed fixing up a bit to make it more
habitable.

Bobby and Mark went off on their almost daily seal
hunt and Jenny and I were working away, chatting as
well as I could manage, and speculating about the old
people who had once lived here. How amused they would
have been, we told each other, if they could see us gathering up their garbage as though it were some precious thing,
and we laughed at the thought of how they must be
laughing at us in whatever world now held them.

Jenny stood up to straighten her back and remained
staring out towards Goodwin Island, as though she saw
something. I was about to ask her what she could see,
when I remember the trick by which I had sent Bobby
off in pursuit of an imaginary polar bear, and said
nothing.

"*Nanook!*" she breathed, hardly above a whisper.

"*Ee?*" I asked, nonchalantly.

"*Marik! Tava! Tukko!*" "Yes, indeed. Over there!
Look!" She spoke with an urgency which left no doubt
as to whether she was fooling or not.

Sure enough, there was a good-sized bear walking along
the crest of the little island or reef which lay between
us and Goodwin Island. It was just about half a mile
away and I didn't think it at all likely that the bear
would get wind of us. Jenny, however, was clearly
frightened, so I went down to get my rifle from the tent.
It was only a hundred yards away right on our way down
to the beach from where we could best watch the bear
through the field glasses and where we would be in
a good position to receive him if he did smell our camp
and come over to investigate.

We ran down to the point where Bobby and Mark used to sit waiting for seals and watched the bear. He strolled slowly along to the north end of the reef and there he paused. His long neck with the small head swung back and forth. He stared over at the cliff where the seagulls nested; he turned again and stared at us.

"He's seen us!" Jenny said in a whisper.

"No! He can't have."

Surely he could neither see us, for we were not moving, nor smell us at that distance.

Slowly the bear advanced till he was at the very edge of the water and then, with a plunge and a splash of white water, he was in and swimming.

Was he coming for us? Jenny crouched down behind the rock windbreak so that he shouldn't see her and I made sure once more that the safety catch was off my rifle and a shell in the breech.

What point do you aim for on a polar bear? I was none too sure. His head, of thick heavy bone, might be a useless attempt, unless you got him in the brain. The heart would be difficult to reach when he was coming right at you. Better try for the head then? Don't shoot too soon, for it's a fairly small target. And don't wait too long, you might not get time to shoot twice.

Meanwhile the bear, all unaware of these plots and plans, was swimming leisurely along, carried by the strong flow of the tide away from our rocky point and out towards the open sea. We watched him through the glasses, turn and turn about, till his head was a small white dot and then he disappeared. He was well out in Hudson Strait by then and where he next made land would be a difficult thing to guess.

Bobby and Mark got back not long afterwards, furious at having missed the bear, full of questions as to what he had done, what we had done, where the bear had gone, and why we hadn't gone after it.

We answered all their questions, sitting round with cups of hot tea and bits of bannock, in a mug-up. Every now and then Bobby would look towards the north-west, hoping against hope that the bear would come back.

On my table in the tent was a small wooden bear that Mark had carved out of a bit of wood for me. I handed it to Bobby.

"Where do you shoot a bear?" I asked.

He pointed to its heart, from the side, and indicated the position of the fore-leg, which should be advanced so as to expose the heart.

Then I turned the little wooden bear so that it was coming right towards him.

"And what now?"

Bobby pointed with my pencil to the bear's head. So that was that, and next time I'd know—if ever there was a next time.

Suddenly, Jenny sprang to her feet, listening.

"*Umiak!*" she whispered.

Then we all stood up and listened.

Yes, no doubt about it. It was the humming, throbbing roar of a motor-boat.

Five minutes later she showed her nose round the point of the little cove and we all ran down to meet her.

Chapter XII

BACK TO PORT BURWELL—AND EMILY

WE all raced down to the water's edge to help them ashore and to see who had come. There was Ernie Lyall, which meant I now had an interpreter, there was Steve, a new Hudson's Bay Company apprentice, and there was Davidee, the Eskimo who had come across with us in the first place, the official engineer.

They told us they had had quite a bad time in coming for us. Ernie Lyall said he had been bailing hard for a good fifteen minutes while going through that big tide-rip.

We had but little time for talking, though, for Jenny soon sprung the big news about our having seen the bear and everybody was eager to start out in pursuit of it now that we had a motor-boat at our command. It was quite possible, they felt, that the bear, seeing nothing but the open sea ahead of him would turn again and make for land, and that would probably put him ashore on the other side of our island.

So we all gulped our tea down, seized our rifles and started off, heading the boat in a north-easterly direction following in the wake of the bear, now so long out of sight. The swift-flowing current carried us along at a great rate and it was only a few minutes till we could swing round to the east and start the circuit of Lacy Island.

I had my binoculars and kept a close watch on any

" It was the conjuror's platform "

" 'Duffle' or blanket cloth is used extensively for clothing "

likely looking spot on land or sea, and everybody was keyed up with anticipation. Soon, however, our course headed south again and still there was no sign of that bear. Not much later we reached the end of the shore line and had to turn west. This carried us into the passage between Lacy and Lawson Islands, which the chart shows to be sprinkled with eddies.

The chart, as usual, was perfectly right, and we buffeted our way through a dirty stretch of water, here smooth and polished like indigo silk, and there churning up in a boiling, seething maelstrom. We had given up all hope of coming up with our bear, and the Eskimos decided to turn into a narrow fjord which splits the north end of Lawson Island.

We conned the motor-boat as far in as we could, half a mile about, and then made her fast while we went farther on up the ravine on foot. The walls were steep and bare, with young gulls standing on narrow rocky ledges staring silently at these strange intruders. We walked quickly along a well-marked trail for another quarter of a mile and came to a sea loch, which filled with salt water at high tide only to lose most of it again as the tide fell.

Here we hoped to find a seal which might have been incautious enough to venture in at high water only to discover that his retreat was cut off till next full tide, but there was no seal to be seen. We picked up a nice big log of driftwood that had been thrown high up on the sides of the ravine, and started back for camp.

It's a little-known place, that dark and echoing ravine on Lawson Island and even on the chart its sides are only dotted in, indicating that it was not explored in detail. For months at a time it sees no human being; for many years at a time it sees no white man. No white man, possibly enough, had ever been there before, and quite possibly none has been since.

L

There was nothing special to see, nothing about it that marked it as different from any other narrow rocky chasm, but it had all the charm, all the fascination of the unexplored, the unrecorded. What might we not find? What mystery might it not conceal? Even now I wonder sometimes was there something there after all? Something that I should have noticed, but missed?

It was getting dusk when we reached the tents and, after dinner, settled down to a discussion of our next move. Did I want them to take me back the next day, or should they come for me again a week or a fortnight later? We debated the weather probabilities and the chances of being stormbound for days, or even weeks, at a time.

Then, asked Ernie Lyall, what about my work? Had I finished or was there still something to be done?

"I've done enough to tell me that these houses were not used by the Tunnits or by any of the old people, but by the grandfathers and the great-grandfathers of the people who live on Killinek to-day," I answered.

"Then there's nothing more to do?"

"Not exactly that. I could go on digging for a few days yet, but I don't think I'd find anything to make me change my opinion."

Bobby had been sitting quietly listening to our discussion, guessing at some of what we said, but saying nothing himself. I turned again to Ernie Lyall.

"Before we started," I said, "I told Bobby that the decision as to whether we should travel or stay should be left in his hands."

"Sure, he told me that."

"Well, tell him what I said about the work and that it's up to him."

Bobby was grinning now, for he felt pretty sure he understood what I had said.

" If the *kablunah* wants to stay another week, it might be all right. We might be able to get back, and we might have to wait many days. If we had to wait very long we might not get back at all. I'll stay and work with him if he wants me to, but I think we should go back, for the season of strong winds is coming very soon."

Ernie told me what Bobby had said, and added that he agreed with him.

"All right. That settles it. We leave here as soon as the tide suits to-morrow."

I made the day's entries in my diary, and wound up my watch. I looked at the barometer. It was dropping rather fast, though the weather had been pleasant enough while we were on our cruise after sea-going bear, and now it looked as if there was wind to come. The Northern Lights were blazing and shimmering as Ernie Lyall and I said good night to each other.

The first stage of my Eskimo summer had passed.

I was up and at work by six the next morning, finishing a sketch of the site, writing my last specimen lists and packing the remaining collections. Then came the striking of our tents and the loading of the motor-boat. Bobby had taken Davidee up to see the old people's house and I caught a few snatches of song. He was demonstrating the use of the conjuror's platform and I could picture the scene clearly enough for he had done just the same for me when first I asked him what it was. Soon they both came back, presenting me with a woman's comb carved from caribou antler and a small skin scraper of quartz which they had found in a little recess between the stones of one of the walls.

I slipped these last two specimens into my pocket, for all my boxes were closed by now and at eleven o'clock that morning we rounded the northern tip of MacColl

Island and started down the west coast, running between it and the long and very narrow unnamed island which lies parallel with it. We were well sheltered from a gusty west wind, but even here it was evident that the weather was growing worse and that crossing Gray Straits might well be out of the question.

We were towing Bobby's boat and soon he began hauling on the tow-line so as to bring the two boats close together, to make himself heard above the roar of our motor.

He held a short consultation with Ernie Lyall.

"Bobby wants to know if he is still to decide about when it is safe to travel."

"Yes, certainly."

"Then he says that we can't cross to-day, and the best place to camp is where he took you to see the other old houses on this island."

That meant going back to the north end of MacColl, and back we had to go. It took us till nearly four in the afternoon, but it was a good camp site, with water and a fair amount of driftwood, though that was less important for a one-night camp, for Bobby used his Primus stove on all such occasions.

We unloaded my larger tent so that I could share it with Ernie Lyall, and prepared for a night of waiting. Jenny improved the hour and started to work cutting out boot soles from the hide of a bearded seal.

This seal is a good deal larger than the ordinary harp seal or *netshek*, and is called *ugjook*. He is a big, powerful brute, with a thick and heavy hide which is used for specially tough jobs, such as skin line, boot soles and extra soles for softer boots.

After we had got the camp in order, the men went out in the motor-boat to see if they could get a seal, but I stayed behind for a last look at the house ruins across the island. They returned in an hour or so with one seal and a report that Bobby had shot no less than three others all of which had sunk before they could reach them.

It was blowing strongly when we went to bed that night, but Bobby was optimistic about the next morning, saying that the wind would either drop or change direction, and that either would suit us well enough.

It was four in the morning when we awoke, broad daylight, but raw and cold with that very early morning feeling which fishermen and autumn duck hunters know so well. The wind had dropped, sure enough, the mists were already rising and it was clear that the fates were with us this time.

We ate a hurried breakfast, packed our gear and by six were under way again. Clear, bright sunlight, the gentlest breeze, and the gleaming white gulls circling above us silhouetted against the blue of the sky. Murres, in threes and fours, flying line ahead low above the water, passed us close by, veering not an inch to right or left, as though they had no idea we existed. They fly fast and look very businesslike about it. They are most handsome and striking black and white birds, breeding in astonishing numbers on the narrow ledges of precipitous cliffs. Here they stand, stiff and erect, bearing a rough resemblance to penguins.

There are no penguins in the Arctic. Perhaps I should apologize for making so bald a statement about what is already well known. My excuse is that a surprising number of cartoonists feel that no Eskimo is complete without his penguin, and one or more of these birds is included in nearly every drawing of the land of the midnight sun, all too often with a totem pole in the background. Penguins are found in the southern polar regions, but never in the north. The polar bear, just to balance things up, refuses to frequent the south pole.

The south end of MacColl Island boasts no less than five protruding fingers of land, separated by four deep bays. At the head of the most westerly of these is a small sea loch, directly connected with the sea at high tide, when it becomes part of the bay itself, and is a lake again when the water drops.

Here we stopped for a mug-up. We got out the Primus and soon had water, dipped from a little stream trickling down the hill to the north-east of us, on the boil and ready for making tea. Jenny handed out hunks of bannock to each, and I dug down into my own stuff for some sweet biscuits, which everybody enjoyed.

We talked about this and that, smoked cigarettes, and went for short walks along the rocky shore. Soon the tide had dropped enough to lock the seaward end of the lake, trapping any seals who might have stayed in too long.

Sure enough, there was a large ranger seal in the lake. As soon as he saw the first one of us he dived and for a long time we could see no more of him. The men strung out along the shore, Bobby, Mark, Davidee, Steve and Ernie Lyall. I was busy with my camera.

After making us wait so long that I, at least, felt sure he must have escaped, the seal was seen again when he came up for air. He was near the outlet of the lake, as though he had been trying to find a way out to the open sea. One of the men fired and in a flash the seal dived again. Minutes later, it seemed, he came up once more somewhere else. He never showed himself for more than a few seconds, just long enough for a gasp of air, and then he was gone. He would swim under the surface as far as he could and, it appeared to us, he would try to make his next breathing place near rocks which scattered the shallow water, or in some such spot where he would not be conspicuous.

He never had a real chance though, for air he must have and every time he rose to breathe he was shot at. After ten or a dozen shots had been fired, he was seen to be hit and soon his body was floating on the surface. One of the men, Bobby I think it was, ran down to the boats and returned with the kayak and the seal was retrieved.

While the kayak was being brought a violent argument broke out between Ernie Lyall and Davidee as to whose shot had proved the lethal one. Ernie was quite sure that he had hit the seal, and Davidee was no less convinced that *he* had. They agreed that each knew the direction from which his shot must have penetrated the animal's body and that they would see who was right after they had examined it.

Soon the seal was brought ashore and the two contestants bent eagerly over the body to see whose shot had been the fatal one. Both were right! There were two bullet holes, each from the expected direction.

Then back to the boats with the kayak and the seal. Both soon were stowed away, the kayak on Bobby's boat and the seal in the after end of the motor-boat. By now the tide was less than half full and the time to attempt to cross Gray Straits once more had come. It was fairly calm and there was no ice to be seen. There was a light wind blowing from the north and so Bobby, whose boat we were still towing, was able to make sail which increased our speed considerably.

In a few minutes we were in the middle of our old enemy the tide-rip. Somehow it didn't seem so rough as it had been before, and we got across with no serious difficulty. Hardly had we reached the other side of this stretch of wild water, however, when our troubles began. Never was such a series of accidents seen before.

First, our motor went dead. Right in the middle of Gray Straits. Bobby, repeating the tactics of our previous crossing, sailed right along so that he could take us in tow. He took up the slack of the tow-rope as he passed so that he might prevent the sudden tension which would come on it once he sailed its length, but in spite of this precaution it parted with a wet twang and left us adrift.

Meanwhile Ernie Lyall had been fiddling with our engine and, just as Bobby was ready to put about and pick us up again, it started with a wholesome roar. We hastily repaired the tow rope, heaved it over to Bobby, and proceeded as before. It looked as if our troubles were over, except that the wind was rising quickly, dark clouds spread over the sky and a heavy rain began to fall. There was a dirty squall coming and Gray Straits is not the best of places in the Arctic or even the sub-Arctic to meet a squall in. There are altogether too many rocks, reefs, shoals and islands scattered about.

The engine now running smoothly, Ernie replaced the front of the wooden engine house, which slid up and down in grooves. This housing was to protect the motor from waves breaking inboard and from spray and was, as a rule, kept shut only in dirty weather and rough water. As we were having both and a "lop" might lick over the gunwale at any moment, killing the motor, this was the right time to use it.

Just as the door was settling neatly into position the bottom of it was caught by the protruding handle of the flywheel, which is used to crank the motor. As a rule, this starting handle fits into a socket in the flywheel, into which it is pulled by a helical spring, as soon as one lets go of it, but occasionally it fails to get home and sticks out like the swords on the axles of Queen Boadicea's chariot wheels, and does just about as much damage.

This time it lifted the sliding door straight up through its grooves and flung it into Ernie Lyall's face, cutting both his lips, the lower one both inside and out, and nearly stunning him. The blood trickled down his face, and he stood swaying, holding on to the engine house to prevent collapsing.

What annoyed Ernie most of all was not the pain, the shock, or that natural resentment against an inanimate thing which does something it shouldn't which we all feel on such occasions, it was the loud, hearty, and quite unrestrained laughter of all the Eskimos, men, women and child. How they love slapstick!

I was sitting crouched down aft, seeking what shelter I could from the wind and the rain, and pleased to discover that whatever I was sitting on was quite pleasantly warm. I paid but little attention to this phenomenon at first and was but barely conscious of it. After the lapse of a short time, it was borne in upon my consciousness that there were no warmed seats on the motor-boat, and that whatever I sat on, tent, sleeping-bag, or roll of hides, ought to be cold.

I looked down to see what was what and found I was sitting on the ranger seal we had shot in the little land-locked bay. The animal heat had not yet left its body, insulated as it was with a layer of blubber, and my sitting still in one spot had allowed the heat to get through. I stayed where I was, and was grateful. Soft and warm, the best seat on the boat.

For a while all went well and I felt that the gods had relented. Then we heard a shout from Bobby. The tiller had come off in his hand. Well, not exactly in his hand, for he had been steering with his legs. He stood up aft with the tiller between his legs and shifted his stance enough to hold it to port or starboard as the circumstances required. Suddenly it had slipped off the rudder head and fallen at his feet.

With Bobby out of control, we had the choice of stopping while he made repairs or dragging him along by main force. We didn't want to stop the motor, for it was hard to tell whether its temperament would let it start again, so we proceeded as before. Bobby dropped his sail and, after a few minutes, had his tiller in place again, and we went on our way.

By now the water was dangerously rough and lops were breaking inboard. We bailed as much and as quickly as we could but, with so much gear on board, we couldn't get at the bottom boards to work effectively and so were obliged to carry a good deal of water which we could not get rid of. The rain was heavier than ever now and the cliffs ahead of us, as well as the Button Islands behind, were completely blotted from our sight.

The only thing we could do was to hold the course we were on, and this was safe enough unless there had been a marked change in the wind, for we had been headed fair for shelter in the lee of the off-shore islands west of Killinek. Soon one of them loomed up before us and we ran into the shelter of its cliffs.

Smooth water, light wind, and the steady downpouring rain. It was a great relief. Looking back we saw in the Straits a confusion of waters in which no boat of our size could hope to live.

Bobby called some joke or other to Davidee, who shouted back an answer with a grin. Rather unusual for Davidee, this grin, for he tends to consider life a somewhat serious business.

"They are saying that we just about didn't make it," explained Ernie. "If we had started fifteen minutes later, we might not have got over at all."

Jenny was still sitting down in the motor-boat crouched behind the engine housing where she had been from the beginning, imperturbable and unafraid, never in the way, always ready to lend a hand if needed. Now she stretched and yawned, grinned and pulled her hands out of the sleeves of her *attigi* into which she had thrust them to keep them warm, as does a Chinese.

"Cigarette?" she asked me. I lit up too, and settled back on my nice warm seal. I don't suppose that I shall ever have occasion to cross Gray Straits, sitting on a dead ranger seal, in an open motor-boat in a squall again.

It rained continuously until we got into Port Burwell, and we were all thoroughly wet and cold. Luckily the tide was now nearly full and we could get through the narrow trickle which runs past the old mission and save ourselves a few miles. We tied up at the little wharf below Number One Warehouse at just about twelve o'clock after six hours on the way.

We unloaded all our stuff immediately, for I was anxious about its getting any wetter than it already was. I was tired and hungry and it seemed a long way from the warehouse up to the living quarters where, I knew, a hot lunch prepared by Tola awaited me.

We had been hard at it since early in the morning; we had hunted seals; we had run tide-rips; we had braved storms. Now I wanted to eat, and then sleep.

Bobby gave a final glance about the boats to make sure all was finished up and shipshape. Satisfied, he turned to me.

"Dance to-night?" he enquired casually.

I had not been contemplating dancing. It had never occurred to me that I might do anything but eat and sleep.

"*Imaha*," I replied guardedly. "Perhaps."

"*Imaha!*" he scoffed. "*Marik!*"

Bobby was right, of course. There was a dance and I was at it. So was Lily and Jenny, and so was Mark—with Emily.

Mark had vanished soon after we landed. True, he did help Bobby with one or two of the heavier bits of stuff, but after that he just disappeared. Bobby grinned when I asked where Mark had got to. It didn't take much guessing, for we had all noticed that the tent that Mark had stared at so intently on that day when we left just three weeks before was still standing on the bank of the little brook. If the tent was still there, Emily would still be there too.

We had a cold, wet rain all that afternoon and it turned into sleet, soggy and heavy, filling all the little crevices into which it drifted and soaking everybody's *kamiks* to a sodden mass, for there's nothing so wet and penetrating as sleet. But the dance was the big thing and it would take a lot more than sleet to keep the people away.

One Eskimo dance is exactly like another and this one was not to be distinguished from its fellows in any way except for a miraculous cocktail, concocted by the Doctor who was pausing here after a trip round Ungava Bay. He, too, took part in the dancing and it was long after midnight when we toasted each other in a final drink and turned into bed. He swears that I was still standing up when I fell asleep and wrapped myself magically in a blanket so that I fell enswathed from head to heels. I don't remember.

Chapter XIII

BOBBY SPENDS HIS WAGES

IT had been a marvellous dance, but there was work to be done the next morning. First of all, I had a long talk with Bobby, with Ernie Lyall acting as my interpreter. There were so many things that I had not understood clearly. Nothing of vital importance, but there had been times when one or the other of us had been struggling for means of expression and the lack of a mutually intelligible medium had been a handicap.

For instance, what had Bobby said about those sheets of mica? Had he meant that the old people actually used them instead of window-panes?

"No," explained Bobby. "I only said that they looked as though one might use them for windows."

"And what were you trying to tell me about the white stone the old people used for knives?"

For answer, Bobby fished in his pocket and brought out a skin scraper chipped from a clear and sugary quartzite.

"This is the kind of stone I meant. We never use it and my father told me that he had never known anybody make a knife or anything else from it. We don't even know where it comes from, only that the old people, the Tunnits, used to use it."

It's quite a distinctive stone, that quartzite, and it was some time later that I learnt that there is a large deposit of it in Nachvak Inlet, farther south along the eastern

173

coast of the Labrador and from which it was traded for many miles north and south. It even turns up in New-foundland and the north-eastern United States.

"And what about the weather?"

"For the next month we shall have much wind and rain. There will be frost almost every night and there will sometimes be snow. There will be a few fine days, too."

"And what about the old houses near your winter home?"

"There are some old houses, older than those we have just left. There are some newer houses too, houses in which people lived only a few years ago."

"Do you remember them?"

"Why, yes. I remember them well, and I can even tell you the names of some of the men who lived in them."

"Good. We shall go and see them as soon as we can get the boat running again."

Yes, the boat had found another way of delaying us. The stuffing box, that temperamental vent where the propellor shaft passes through the hull on its journey from the motor to the screw, was leaking. It is filled with cotton waste soaked with thick oil and this packing is then put under pressure by means of a tightening screw so as to make a watertight job, but almost any stuffing box would much rather leak than not.

This one had been weeping most of the way across Gray Straits. Not badly, but enough to show that if it were not attended to soon it might just as well not be there at all.

It wasn't much of an undertaking, but it took the best part of a day and that gave me time to overhaul my clothes and equipment. I had decided to leave behind, at the Post, anything that I should not need at the new camp site, with a view to reducing the work of moving. Among the things to be left behind were all the specimens I had collected on the Button Islands.

It was getting towards the end of August and the weather was a good deal colder than it had been only a short time before. I decided that I might as well get Tola to make me another duffle parka, or rather an *attigi,* a garment to go inside my parka and provide additional warmth.

She took no measurements, just looked me over with a calculating and quite unemotional eye, and set to work. It was ready the next evening and fitted perfectly, of course. Tola would have been deeply ashamed if it had not.

Then came further discussions with Bobby. For one thing he had, he presumed, a good deal coming to him in wages.

"Yes, quite a good deal. Three weeks' pay, at the least."

"And there will be still more to come."

This was put in the form of a statement, rather than as a question.

"Yes, there will be so much for every day that we work together."

That was a little convention we both liked to abide by. Bobby was not working for me, he was working with me, because he liked to oblige a friend. For a reasonable consideration, naturally.

"Then, may I get things from the Company store with the wages I have already earned?"

"Yes, you can get whatever you want, up to the number of skins you have earned. I will speak to the manager and he will give you whatever you need."

"Good! Now I shall have a telescope, for that is a thing I have always wanted."

That was Bobby's first purchase, and the only one which really interested him. For years he had wanted that telescope, and now, at last, here was his opportunity.

The telescope hung in its polished brown leather case, high out of reach, symbolically high it seemed, far above the shelves behind the counter in the store.

Bobby pointed to it without a word. The post manager got a stool and balanced himself cautiously on it. He reached down the telescope and placed it on a lower shelf. Then he got down from the stool and dusted the case on the leg of his trousers, restoring the shine to the brown leather.

Bobby stood patiently watching these things. He had waited so long that he could surely wait a minute longer. Only the involuntary lifting of his hands and a twitching of his fingers revealed how difficult it was to resist the impulse to snatch it from the slow-moving *kablunah's* hands.

"It is a good telescope," said the post manager. "It will cost you many fox skins."

Bobby snorted.

He had known the price of that telescope longer than the post manager had, for he was a new-comer, comparatively speaking, and the telescope had hung there long before his arrival.

The post manager unbuckled the leather cap at the end and drew out the instrument itself. The shining brass joints were a little stiff after so long a period of lying idle and he pulled and twisted them gently to stretch the tube out to its full length.

Still Bobby waited.

At last the post manager was satisfied and he raised the telescope to his eye, adjusting the focus as he brought it to bear on the hillside near the old coal dump just across the harbour.

" Tents are low down to the ground reducing wind resistance "

Eskimo children look surprisingly like Japanese dolls

"It's a good telescope," he said again quietly, as he gave it, at long last, into Bobby's aching hands.

In his turn, Bobby scrutinized the far shore, now and then making a minute shift in the length of the barrel. He walked over to the door where he could see more.

Now the cooler outside air frosted the object lens and the image grew faint and blurred. He turned to me after looking at it and his expression said clearly enough that there was something wrong.

"It's the cold," I explained. "Leave it out in a cold place in the winter, don't bring it in the house where it will get warm, or that will happen again."

I wiped the lens carefully and returned it to him. One glance satisfied him, and he put it back in its case. I had an idea that he wanted to be away from the store before he really explored its possibilities, away from the watching, curious eyes of the manager and all the others.

Later I was able to give him some idea of how to clean and care for that telescope and it is, I feel quite sure, one of his most valued, and valuable, possessions.

What happened to the rest of his wages was a matter of less importance to Bobby. Jenny and Lily, more especially Jenny, would see to it that their stores of food were properly replenished, that there was ample tobacco, and that they had all the household goods they needed. No rubbish was bought; indeed, there was very little rubbish there for them to buy. Competition, which makes some trading posts carry all sorts of cheap junk, designed to catch the eye of the unsophisticated, was absent from Port Burwell and necessary, or nearly necessary, articles only were for sale.

I was interested to discover that some, at any rate, of the natives on Killinek Island count their money, on the few occasions when counting is necessary, in shillings and pence, rather than in dollars and cents. It is a relic of

M

the old days of the whalers, most of whom came from Scotland.

At last the stuffing box was stuffed and the boat reasonably watertight again. The afternoon was fine next day, so we started out for a tour of investigation. It is about six miles in a straight line from Port Burwell to the new site at the south-west corner of McLelan Strait, a body of water which cuts through the northern tip of the Labrador and makes Killinek the island it is, rather than a bit of the mainland as it probably once was. Killinek means "that which is farthest out," a sort of Eskimo rendering of *ultima thule*.

These Straits are about fifteen miles long and, at the two narrowest parts, not more than two hundred yards wide. It's a long and narrow defile, with hills on the two sides fifteen hundred feet high or more. It is deep, presumably, though it has never been sounded to my knowledge, and reasonably straight. There is a swift and vicious current and he would be a brave skipper, and a foolhardy one, who would venture this as a short cut to avoid going round by Cape Childey. It has been done in small boats, but it's much too narrow for a steamer, and a sailing-boat would have no room to tack and would meet rough winds and sudden gusts at the mouth of every little valley. All in all, it's a good place to keep away from.

Two Moravian missionaries, Kohlmeister and Kmoch, passed through McLelan Strait in 1811 in an open *umiak*, an Eskimo boat of skins stretched on wood, with four native families. They were on their way from the east coast of Labrador to Ungava Bay, where they hoped to found a new mission, and perhaps another near Killinek. Later that summer, they returned by the same route. They passed close by the site we were going to visit, and reported the presence of natives in the district.

In 1906 another German, Bernhard Hantzsch, who was staying at the new mission established at Killinek over a hundred years later, went through the Strait with a single Eskimo companion and returned by the same route. They were storm bound for a good deal of the time, and Hantzsch gives a vivid account of the dangerous currents and whirlpools.

Bobby knew all about the dangers of McLelan Strait for he had been born and brought up here. He called it Ikkerasak, which means "the passageway." Just at the moment, he knew, the tide would be rushing through at a great rate and he took advantage of a sort of back door. Parallel with McLelan Strait is Tunnussaksuk, which means "turned about" or something of that sort, a blind alley, long and narrow, in which the tide is much less violent.

Here he ran into a little cove, safe and secure, where we could come close alongside the shore in the motor-boat. The old house ruins were on the other side of the peninsula dividing the straits from the inlet. It was about six hundred yards across to the little promontory on which they stood and our path lay over a rocky plateau, some fifty feet or so above sea level.

There proved to be several old houses here, some of them apparently a good deal older than those at the site on the Button Islands. There were also a number of old graves, but they had all been broken open long ago. There has been a native village here for many years, for it is a place where the sea does not freeze over even in the hardest winters. As a result, seals come here to breathe all the year round and the hunters are able to get them when other people, hunting seals at the edge of the sea ice, have no such opportunities.

We could stay only half an hour or so, for the heavy tide would be against us all the way back once we got out of the shelter of our blind alley, but I saw enough in that time to know that this was a site which might well repay the work we spent on it.

One of the house ruins, square in cross-section rather than round, I marked down for the first to be opened and then, after a glance inside Bobby's winter home, a small wooden shack, it was time to get back to the Post at Port Burwell.

The tide was swirling and boiling along and we had not gone very far when our rudder came adrift and left us pretty well helpless for a few minutes. One of the several natives we had with us seized an oar and steered with it while we made the best of our way into a little bay on the opposite side of McLelan Strait.

Fortunately the rudder lines still held the rudder fast to the boat and so it was a fairly simple matter to slip it back on to the pintle once we were in still water. Then out into the current and there, swimming alongside of us and bucking the tide in the same way, were three large —what? Porpoises, or grampus, or belugas? I never found out. They are large mammals, as much as ten feet long and perhaps more, and they sigh as they come up to breathe. It is a fairly quiet sound, yet it can be heard for a long way. We were to hear it many times in the days to come, for McLelan Strait seems to be a regular highway for them and almost every day we were to see one or more as they passed through.

Soon every rifle in the boat was blazing away at them, for one of these beasts provides a good deal of dog feed, but apparently none of them was hit for there was no bloodstain in the water. We certainly killed none.

Another dance that night! There seems to be no point of satiation for the Eskimo when it's a matter of dancing. This time we had the handkerchief dance, which I had not seen before.

It was started by a girl who, carrying an ordinary bandanna handkerchief, walked in an aimless, serpentine fashion about the open floor space, without apparent regard for the music. After making two circuits, she threw the handkerchief to a young man, who caught it and then rose and fell in close behind her, almost in a lock-step, holding the back of her dress just above the waist.

This couple made two circuits of the floor and then the boy threw the handkerchief to one of the many girls who were sitting on the side lines, watching the dance. She rose and hitched on behind the boy, held the handkerchief for two more circuits and then she threw it to the boy she selected.

They kept on in this way till just about everybody was up, walking round and round the room in a long snake, men and women alternating. Then the last one in the line, a boy as it happened, broke off, took his place in the middle of the floor and the others formed a cirle about him.

Here he danced slowly round with the bandanna formed into a sling which he held by the two opposite corners, the loop of it behind his head and the ends brought forward like horns. When he came opposite the girl he liked best, he flipped the handkerchief forward and caught her in the loop, and dragged her into the circle with him. Now he left her there and went back to his own seat, leaving her the bandanna with which to catch her own true love. So one by one they went back to their seats till there were only three or four left to make the "circle," when it all suddenly broke up in laughter.

As a dance, it wasn't much, but it is one that the boys often ask for and which the girls pretend to be too shy to take part in, probably because they have to choose and be chosen, quite an embarrassing thing for a modest maiden. There was loud laughter at some of the choices made and it took Jenny a long time to make up her mind to catch me, the *kablunah*, but at last she ventured and all the women howled their appreciation of the joke.

There was a marvellous display of Northern Lights that night as we walked back to the residence. They are very common in this latitude, even more so than farther north, for the maximum number of displays in a year is to be found in about latitude 60, which is just where we were. Here there are well over a hundred displays annually, whereas New York gets an average of ten and London perhaps six, and pretty feeble affairs at that.

They are old stuff to the Eskimos, of course, and they pay very little attention to them for they have already been explained to their complete satisfaction. They are the ghosts of the dead playing football with an old walrus skull, and everybody knows that, so there's no need to discuss it further.

Almost anywhere in the North there are great arguments to be heard as to whether the Northern Lights make a noise or not. Some say they do and others, just about as numerous, say they do not or that they, at any rate, have never heard them. There are lots of interesting by-paths and sidelights to the argument, for those who insist that they have heard them, all seem to agree as to the kind of noise they make, and this with no possible collaboration, for people as far apart as Alaska and the Labrador agree that when they do hear the Northern Lights, and they are all willing to admit that they are usually silent, but when they do hear them they make a noise like the rustling of silk.

Another belief is that if you whistle loudly during a display of the Lights, they will respond with the silk-like noise and you can hear the answer plainly on a still night. Scientists point out that these clouds of electrons, if they are electrons, forming the Lights are about two hundred miles above the surface of the earth and that if they do make a noise, which is to them quite incredible in the first place, it is so far away that we couldn't possibly hear it.

In Cartwright, farther south along the Labrador coast, I was told that the Lights sometimes come down so low to the earth that they are actually between the spectator and the near-by hills and one old man told me that he had actually seen them between himself and his boat shed, down at the water's edge. When the Lights are as low as this, they warn you, you must be careful not to walk into them, for it's sure death if you do.

There was still another dance that evening, but this time I passed it up. My heels were stiff and sore for, the night before, I had danced in my soft-soled sealskin kamiks and the low heels had strained my Achilles tendons without my perceiving it at the time. The next morning I could hardly walk. I hobbled along like an old man and all my Eskimo friends, passing me as they went about their various affairs, would turn and gaze after me in amazement. I rubbed and massaged the ailing tendons and, towards evening, they grew slightly more flexible.

I was reminded of my first long trip on skis when the long heavy tendons on the inner side of my thighs grew so stiff that I could only hobble like a greybeard when I went into the chemist's shop for some liniment.

Next morning, though we were all ready to go, a high wind made it inadvisable to set out so I spent some time straightening out my accounts to date and then went for a walk with Jenny in search of graves. There are a good many in the neighbourhood, though most of them have been opened at one time or another, and there are seldom any grave goods to be found cached near them. About the middle of the afternoon, when the tide was high, the wind dropped and we suddenly made up our minds to start off. In spite of everything we could do, it was nearly five o'clock before we got away and we had to stop to pick up Bobby who was at home in the little cove where he usually stayed when he was at the Post.

It took but a few minutes for him to strike his tent, pack everything on board, and get under way again and we reached our new site at about seven in the evening without incident, except that when we were well out of sight of Port Burwell we saw a motor-boat headed our way. There were a number of natives in it and I could see that my family wondered who they were and wanted to stop for a chat with the new-comers, so I gave a nod to Davidee and he shut off the motor. In a few minutes they were alongside and proved to be old acquaintances from Fort Chimo on their way to Killinek. I was pointed out and explained, but could take little part in the conversation. Bobby predicted, rather wistfully, that there would be a big dance that night!

Little Jimmy was the first ashore when we got to our destination, and with a good reason. He is a clean child as far as his personal habits are concerned and retires out of sight for his natural functions, something which some of the older Eskimos feel a quite needless refinement.

His garments are devised in a simple but effective way, common among Eskimo children. There is no fly in the front of his trousers; there is instead a slit which extends well round to the back. When he stands up, Jimmy's trousers are decorously closed, but if he squats down, everything opens up automatically, and there are no obstructions to prevent the gratifying of his desires. It saves a lot of running round to be unbuttoned and rebuttoned.

One of the difficulties of travelling, with a crowd of people of mixed sexes in an open boat, is the complete lack of sanitary facilities of even the crudest kind. The stern of the boat offers the only solution possible and all hands gaze earnestly ahead while the stern is in use. Even the steersman, if the boat is tiller-rigged, knows nothing of what is going on beside him. Missionaries' wives have been heard to say that they have found it embarrassing at times, especially in rough weather.

We put up only the larger of my tents that evening, leaving the job of getting camp shipshape till the next morning. Bobby pitched his where it had so often stood before, though he was less than half a mile from his winter house. I think they prefer the light and airiness of a tent to the comparatively stuffy closed wooden shack.

Near by was a little freshwater pond from which we got our drinking water, or at any rate some of it. There were many kinds of beasts living in it and I had to filter it through a handkerchief before it was fit to use. I pickled some of my catch and a colleague wrote a learned paper on the inhabitants of our water supply some months later.

Farther away, a few hundred yards to the east, was a much better source, for here a stream cascaded down the side of a hill and there was an abundance of clear cold water. Usually I preferred to walk over here with a pail to get a day's supply of drinking water, but Jenny used the pond water for washing and cooking purposes.

Chapter XIV

NUNAINGOK—THE HIDDEN LAND

THERE was one thing about the new site that suited Mark very well and that was our being nearer to the Post. Not that he could go and see Emily just whenever he wanted to, for that would require the use of the sailboat which needed two men to handle it properly, but he at least knew that he wasn't as far away as he had been.

While we were in Port Burwell, between operations on the two sites, he had spent as much time with her as he conveniently could and apparently his rival had not been able to make very much progress during Mark's absence on the Button Islands, for he and Emily had become a recognized and acknowledged pair at the dances.

Mark had discovered that I had a couple of cartons of cigarettes on hand and whenever he ran out of them, which was frequently, he would wait an opportunity when we were alone and ask me for a package.

"*Cigarette?*" he would ask, with an enquiring intonation, as much as to say, "I don't suppose you happen to have any to spare."

"*Marrik!*" I would answer cheerfully, "Sure thing!" and I'd hand over a package of twenty-five. I believe the assumption was that the cost of the cigarettes would be deducted from his wages, but Mark clearly hoped that at least some of them would be overlooked in the final reckoning. When that day came and the last wages due were credited to Bobby for the whole family, Mark made no mention of this little matter, and I ignored it too.

He had an engaging smile and would dribble and chuckle with appreciation whenever there was anything to be amused about, which was quite often for they all loved a joke, except perhaps Lily who found it was just too much trouble to figure out what there was to be amused about.

Our first morning at the new site was spent in putting up my smaller tent. This proved to be quite an undertaking, for the wind was more violent than any we had had so far, though a mere nothing to what was to come. Three guy ropes snapped soon after the full strain came on them and we had to tie in new ones.

Larger and larger boulders were selected as anchor stones for the guys and more and more stones would be piled in front of the anchor stone to help it keep its footing. The usual arrangement was to place two large stones, weighing about a hundred pounds each, side by side and about a couple of inches apart. The guy rope would be passed through the opening between them and tied round an even larger stone laid behind the first two. On top of the triangle thus formed would be placed a fourth stone, as large as one could lift. It made a pretty solid and heavy pyramid, weighing perhaps as much as four hundred pounds. More than once I have seen the guy rope pull the anchor stone right through the pyramid, simply by the pressure of the wind on the side of the tent.

The walls and ends of the tent flapped and worried continuously, bellied out, or in, like sails in a strong wind and the three-inch spruce tent poles bent visibly under the strain. It was remarkable that the tents could stand at all and no wonder that they occasionally gave it all up and collapsed, a wet and soggy mass, on top of their contents.

Bobby's tent stood better than either of mine, probably because of its superior design. First of all, it sat lower down to the ground, thus reducing the resistance it offered to the wind and, in the second place, there were no flat sides or ends, for its outline was oval. There was a two-foot wall, but this was too low to cause much trouble while yet giving enough head room inside the tent.

It had guy ropes all round, attached to stones just as mine were, and there were also large stones piled along the curtain of the tent where the side wall reached the ground. Bobby's tent came down only once or twice while I was with them; by reason of the wind, that is. Little Jimmy would knock a tent pole galley west every now and then and either threaten the whole business with collapse, or actually succeed in bringing it right down. Lily's internal struggles to right matters on one such occasion were well worth watching.

One admirable thing about our new site was that it was much drier than the one on the Buttons and we could go for a walk without getting ourselves soaking wet up to the knees.

We had many a good time on these walks in the vicinity of our camp. There were so many things to see and, now that the autumn was well on its way, there were all the changes in the vegetation to take note of. The blueberries were ripe and sweet. There were not many of them and they were hardly worth picking except where they were unusually numerous. Here and there one would find a little gravel bank, about waist high, where they grew and then they could be picked without stooping. This is an important consideration in the sub-Arctic where the bushes are seldom more than three or four inches high, being dwarfed by the inclement climate.

In the old days, before the white men came, the Eskimos used very little vegetable food. In the spring they were always glad to chew on green leaves and tender buds and they would also eat bits of fresh seaweed gathered at low tide. In the summer, they ate a few sorrel leaves, pleasant for their acid taste, and the semi-digested mosses and lichens in a caribou's stomach were sometimes sprinkled with oil and eaten as a salad. For the most part, however, their diet was meat.

There were dwarf birches to be seen too, two or three inches high perhaps, but complete trees as far as leaves and fruit were concerned. Some were a little larger but, large or small, the little birch leaves turn yellow in the autumn and the leaves of other plants turn scarlet and orange just as they do a thousand miles to the south, some six weeks later.

Later that morning, having got the camp into some sort of order, Bobby and I walked over to the old igloos again to examine them more carefully. The one farthest to the south had the appearance of being older than any of the others and I had already decided that it should be the first to be investigated. Farther to the north was another, which Bobby insisted was very old, but I was not at all sure on what grounds. There was lush green grass growing within the ruined walls and there were bits of European stuff lying about the surface, such as earthenware and iron.

Bobby's story was that this was a very old house which had been cleaned out and re-occupied by a family a good many years ago, and that he remembered the incident himself. So this was marked down for the second job as it seemed to offer some chance of finding older material in its lower levels.

Then back to camp for lunch, to tighten up all the guy ropes on all three tents, move the anchor stones back to the places from which they have been pulled, and then over to the dig again, this time with Jenny to see what there was in the district in the way of graves. We found several, some of them quite obviously recent and others much older.

Among the recent ones was a very small grave, certainly that of a child, and Jenny asked me not to touch it.

"Whose grave is it?" I asked, having assured her that I had no intention of opening any recent graves.

She mentioned the name of a young girl.

"But it can't be; she's at the Post at Killinek."

"Her baby."

"Oh. And who was the father?"

"A *kablunah*," said Jenny simply, and that was that.

There are a good many half-breed children in the eastern Arctic, and a good many half-breed adults too, and have been for many years, since the days of the first whaling ships, in fact. Here and there one will see an Eskimo with curly hair and a swarthy complexion and a Portuguese look about him. Others show white influence in the form of a complexion even lighter than the average Eskimo, who is normally about as dark as an Italian perhaps, though with less of the olive tint. Some of the whaling ships, one perceives, also had some Negro deck hands or cooks aboard.

There is apparently no social disapproval of these children of mixed descent. They take a normal place in their society, are brought up as Eskimos and, in most cases, are unmindful of their paternity. Some of them know that they are half white, or that one of their parents was half white, but they dress and speak and behave and, in every way, live like Eskimos and seem quite content to do so.

of adhesive was all that was needed to pull the two edges into place. Lily's operation was all over.

Now there was Jenny's knee, but that was not very serious. Next came Mark, with a boil on his back. It was hardly ripe and there was nothing much to be done about it.

"Come back to-morrow," I told him, "and I'll open it up for you."

There was no sign of Mark the next morning or the next, but I could see that the boil was hurting him and that he didn't put much weight on the handle of his shovel when we were working on the igloo ruin.

After lunch, I called Mark over to my tent and asked him to show me the boil.

"All gone," he explained casually.

"Let me see then."

Reluctantly Mark pulled up his shirt and revealed his boil. It was a beauty; deep purple with a bright red margin round it and a high shining centre. I opened up my medical kit and took out a lancet.

"*Auka!*" objected Mark, just as Lily had done.

"*Ee!*" I insisted. "*Mikkiuk!*" and showed him how very small indeed was the incision I intended making. It was but a grudging assent he gave, but he turned and bowed his back.

It hardly needed cutting at all, for the first touch of the sharp edge brought a gush of thick yellow pus and, after but the slightest pressure on the surrounding tissues, the core of the boil stood out clear and distinct. I lifted it out with a small pair of forceps.

Mark examined it with interest and then I held a shaving mirror so that he could see the damage for himself. I washed it up and put a dressing on it, while Mark grinned broadly with satisfaction.

"*Peeouyuk?*" I asked. "Feels better?"

N

"Peeouyuk marrik!" and then, quite as an after-thought, "Cigarette?"

Work was going well on the new igloo. There had been a few bits of iron and pottery lying about in the grass on the surface, but once we got the turf stripped off there was no further trace of European influence. Almost at once we found pieces of flaked and chipped quartzite such as the Tunnits had used, but none of these was of a type indisputably Tunnit. However there was no need to despair or to abandon the igloo, for there was still a lot of digging to be done in it.

The original excavation must have been fairly roomy. It measured roughly twenty feet square or a little less and the doorway, six feet long, faced the waters of McLelan Strait. The back wall of the room was steeply dipping bedrock and the side walls were merely the loose gravel in which the house had been dug.

Since its abandonment the dwelling-place had been filled with sand, blown in from an adjacent area of coarse loose soil, and it was excellent stuff to dig in. It was perfectly easy to get a clean-cut vertical face and to work this back gradually with small hand trowels, thus examining every cubic inch of the soil.

Here and there were largish stones, about the size of a man's head, but they were not in any regular arrangement, and it seemed probable that they had formed part of the roof rather than of the walls, for there was no trace of any standing internal wall anywhere, except lining the two sides of the entrance passage.

Soon it became evident that we had got down below the layer in which artifacts were to be found, but there was reason to suspect that there might be a lower stratum under the sand. How far down this might be we could not tell, but it seemed improbable that it should be far.

So, starting right at the entrance, we drove a trench

through the igloo from front to back, deep enough to be sure to get down to undisturbed soil. The sand stood straight and clean, just as it was cut by the edge of the shovel and, except for an occasional stone, the walls of the trench were perfect.

There wasn't very much, after all. The lower culture layer, when we found it, was hardly a layer at all, just a few scattered odds and ends, at various heights and not all lying at the same level as they might have been if they were the debris of a definite period of occupation. We found a whetstone, a flake of mica, a piece of worked slate (and that's certainly not Tunnit!), a rubbed slate point (nor that!), a quartzite chip, a small slate knife, and a flake of quartz. Not Tunnit after all.

Well, we had three weeks left and there was still the other igloo which we had decided to dig. We had one more chance. Next day we would tacke the north igloo of Site Four.

Jenny had been working at a pair of new sealskin boots and she presented them to me one morning, after having made them a little smaller. She still was impressed by the size of my feet apparently. My old ones, which I had on at the time, were wet and very slippery, for sealskin, when it is thoroughly wet, becomes almost like a thick jelly though still amazingly tough and quite waterproof.

I tried to get a good grip on the heel of one of my boots so as to pull it off but, try as I might, the skin would slip out of my fingers again and again.

"*Tsiro!*" exclaimed Jenny. "Half a minute!"

She bent down and seized the slippery heel of my boot firmly in her teeth, grabbed me below the knees and pulled! Off came the boot and, a moment later, the other was off, too, in the same way. It may have been a mark of peculiar affection; it may have been nothing more than the usual solution of a common problem;

at any rate it was new to me and somewhat breath-
taking.

The Eskimos use their teeth much more than we do.
More than most of us could, in fact, for their teeth are
usually amazingly perfect, whereas many white people
to-day have weak and diseased teeth. Diet makes the
difference. I have seen an Eskimo lean over the side of
a boat and seize one flipper of a dead seal in his teeth, the
other in both his hands, give a mighty heave with his
back, and land the seal in the boat. They use their teeth
in untying tight knots in wet rawhide thongs as a matter
of course and also for holding things still while some
operation is being performed on them. Still another use
of the teeth is to bite the dogs' ears as a punishment for
some fault. The dogs don't like it.

Mark went out one day and shot three fish with his ·22.
They had been swimming lazily about in the little cove
near the dig where a small freshwater stream runs in past
Bobby's winter house. Bobby got nine cod-fish by jigging
and the whole dozen were lying in the grass beside their
tent. Once, when I glanced at them in passing, I noticed
that all their eyes had gone. Fish eyes are regarded as
great delicacies and they had been sucked out of the
sockets by somebody as a special treat.

Jigging is a common method of catching codfish.
There is not much sport in it, but the Eskimo doesn't go
fishing as a recreation, he does it to make his living. The
method is to let a large hook down to the bottom where
the cod lie in numbers. There are certain banks which
the fish frequent and the Eskimos have a pretty good idea
of just where to go for them. The hook is quite plain
and unbaited. When it is felt to have touched the bottom
it is jerked up a foot or so fairly smartly and then let
down again.

This jigging of the hook up and down is kept up till

some unlucky fish is snagged. It may be in the gills, or near the tail, in the belly, almost anywhere, and up he is hauled, the victim of his inadvertent passing by just as the hook was snatched upwards.

Later in the day, Bobby went out after game again and this time he got a young bearded seal. This he flensed himself instead of leaving it to Jenny and Lily, and the method he adopted was not the usual one of slitting it down the belly. Instead he made two circular incisions, one round the whole body just below the flippers and the other a couple of feet farther down. This cylinder of skin he peeled off carefully without cutting it; then he scraped it clean and set it aside for a short time. His purpose was to make it into a strong thong, using a helical cut which would give him a long continuous strip, to be made into dog traces for the winter.

He had done a good deal of the work on the seal's carcass on shore near where he had shot it, and had carried the various portions in the interior of his kayak after dismembering it, all except the internal organs, which he washed and carried on the deck just in front of him.

As a result of this cargo, the inside of the kayak was smeared liberally with blood and offal and had to be washed. Bobby carried it up on the gravelly beach and poured in two or three buckets of salt water. He and Mark then picked up the kayak and sloshed the water about inside it till the interior was clean again. Then they turned it over and held it with the bow lower than the stern. Of course, all the water ran down towards the bow and then Bobby pulled out a small wooden plug. In a minute or two all the blood-stained water had run out, he turned the kayak right side up, replaced the plug, and it was all ready for use again.

This little plug, which is much like a pencil in size and shape, is in the very front of the kayak on the upper side of the deck. Its true function is not readily detected and, although I had noticed it before, I had always assumed that it was merely a part of the wooden framework of the kayak.

I was surprised to notice that neither Bobby nor Mark had much hesitation in stepping on the deck of the kayak even when it was lying up on the beach. Apparently the frame is strong enough to support a man, though they do avoid subjecting it to this strain more often than necessary.

That night I had some little trouble with my gasoline stove. The generator appeared to be plugged and I decided that I must take it off and replace it by one of the spares. I was going to discard the old generator when Bobby asked me if he might have it. I gave it to him, of course, but asked him what earthly use it was since he had no stove to use it in.

"It's still good," he said, "or I can mend it."

"It's no good if you have no stove."

"How much does such a stove cost?"

"About twenty dollars."

"That is only two fox skins. I shall buy such a stove. I have seen you use it and it is good."

Then a bright idea struck him; or had it been in his mind from the beginning?

"Will you sell me your stove when you go away on the *umiajuak*?"

"No, for it is not my stove. It is a government stove. I cannot sell it. If it was broken and of no use I could throw it away."

"Perhaps it will break some day. Then you will throw it away?"

"Yes."

"Good. I will come with you and help you throw it away."

Little Jimmy was quite used to me by now, of course, and often selected me as a playmate if he could catch me when I wasn't obviously busy with something else. One of his favourite games was "talking" with the *kablunah.* He would rattle off an amazing string of nonsense syllables and wait patiently while I answered in kind. Then would come another volley, shorter this time and ending with a rising inflection. Obviously a question. I would answer shortly, sounds meaning nothing, but uttered in a quiet and serious tone, such as used by two wordly wise old men, discussing the obvious but proud of their sagacity and of their ability to agree on such deep things.

Jimmy would respond in kind, catching the tone precisely. After a pause, another long statement and then another reply and so our endless and senseless conversations would go on to the unbounded amusement of his parents as well as Jenny and Mark.

I never could quite fathom Jimmy's understanding of this game. Was he pretending to talk English? Did he think that I was answering him in English? Or was he just amusing himself by pretending to talk?

When he did say something serious, I had the greatest difficulty in following his meaning for he still used a good deal of Eskimo baby-talk which, surely, nobody but his own immediate family and friends could ever hope to understand. However, some of his remarks were comprehensible enough as when he called to me "*Tukko! Tukko!*" meaning "Look!" or "Watch!" while he performed some feat of skill or daring.

We were working in the last igloo all one day, finding a fair number of specimens and, as they turned up, Bobby, or Jenny, or I, would hold up what we had just found and name it. Added to its name we used the suffix "*venek*" which has the force of "that which once was."

Thus *ulu-venek* means that which once was a knife, or an old knife, *koodleevenek*, an old lamp, and so on.

This went on for some time and our finds were laid out in a row side by side on a convenient ledge. Jimmy, pretty well bored, was watching us at work and now and then he tried to help, though he was never allowed to do any actual digging. This was a sore spot with him, for he was quite confident that he could dig just as well as the next fellow.

Determined to make his contribution, he picked up a burnt-out match I had thrown down but a minute before and added it to the pile of specimens.

"*Matchesi-venek*," he announced casually, and turned to seek yet other treasures.

Noonaingok is the Eskimo name of the new site, and it means "the hidden place" or, more correctly perhaps, "the hidden land." Kohlmeister and Kmoch noted the settlement when they passed by there in 1811, and it was examined by Dr. Robert Bell in 1877. Seven years later, A. R. C. Selwyn was there, when the meteorological station was established at Port Burwell and it was still inhabited at that time.

It is, indeed, a hidden place, for one might pass close along the eastern shore of Ungava Bay without knowing of its existence. A good place to camp in, for there are many seals at all seasons of the year, there are fish to be had, and from there access to the inland areas where caribou are to be found is easy. One-eyed Bobby knew what he was about when he decided that he would stick, even if he was the sole remaining inhabitant.

Chapter XV

BOBBY GOES HUNTING AGAIN

WE soon settled down into our customary routine in our new camp. There was the excavating to be done in the igloo, slowly and carefully, and this was much easier now that everybody understood just how I wanted them to do it. It was no longer necessary to keep warning them to work slowly, or to supervise each shovelful of debris.

There were specimens to record; they all had to have a preliminary cleaning; some had to have temporary repairs; numbers for them had to be written on slips of coloured paper which could easily be distinguished from the newspaper each was wrapped in, the numbers being in pencil, for ink blurs if it gets wet.

There were daily notes to be entered in the journal, a record of the progress of the excavation, and comments on the evidence obtained as we went along. There were excursions in the neighbourhood, both as a means of recreation and to make sure that nothing of importance had been overlooked. There were specimens of local rocks and minerals to collect for colleagues in the Museum back at home, plant specimens, both land and marine, and many other odd jobs.

After working on the igloo all one morning we got back to camp for lunch and found Bobby's tent down, and neither of mine likely to stand much longer. We had a good deal of trouble in getting his up again in the rising gale and, after it was all over, Jenny told me that my smaller one had come down once during the morning and that she and Lily had put it up again.

The wind was increasing rapidly and loose sand was blowing along forcefully, almost cutting bare skin. The tents were bellying more than ever before and I could hardly believe that they would stand through the night. Rather than risk a collapse while I was sleeping, I moved my cot into the larger tent, added new stones to the already large pyramids holding the guy ropes and strung a heavy line, Bobby's tow-rope in fact, from my ridge pole to a mooring stone almost a hundred feet ahead. This gave me an elastic, strong support which would take up a lot of strain and it was this, I am convinced, that kept the tent standing through that night.

We tried going out for a walk in the latter part of the afternoon, keeping in sight of camp in case of any trouble, but it was so unpleasant that we soon returned. I took refuge in Bobby's tent, where the wind seemed to be making less noise, and we amused ourselves with string figures. Work in the igloo would have been impossible, for we had had a demonstration that very morning of how the wind had filled it up with sand in the years past. It was a regular sandstorm, so thick that one could not keep one's eyes open, or only at the risk of having them filled with the cutting, gritty particles of sand.

Bobby did a few string figures himself, but he was not so adept at it as was Jenny. Well aware of the reluctance to let young men make string figures, I took the loop of cord and handed it over to Mark, as much as to say, "Let's see what you can do."

Mark grinned in an embarrassed way, and glanced at Bobby. Bobby grinned too, but there was a trace of a serious note in his voice as he turned to me and, partly in words and partly by example, showed me what they feared might happen if Mark attempted to show me some. As soon as they saw that I understood, Mark handed the string back to Jenny and everybody breathed freely again. No bad luck for Mark, as a result of risking himself in this finger-entangling game!

It is a belief related to the fundamental principles of sympathetic magic, which holds that like produces like. Thus, if you want rain, you ask a priest to pour water on the ground with the appropriate rituals and words; if you wish to injure your enemy, make a clay image of him, or a wax one, and stick pins in it so as to make him suffer as his image suffers; if you wish to keep your hands out of dangerous snarls, see to it that they are never caught even in innocent ones. It's all perfectly logical, if you accept the fundamental premises; most of us do not accept them; most Eskimos do.

Later on I produced some paper and pencils and set them to drawing pictures. Jenny, as usual, proved to be the most intelligent, though her skill as a draughtsman was nothing to boast of. On one of the sketches she drew she wrote LILY in English letters, but there was very little resemblance between the portrait and the sitter.

When we were on the Buttons I had drawn a landscape with coloured crayons. It was no masterpiece, carelessly and hastily done, more to amuse little Jimmy than anything else, but Jenny had asked me if she might keep it, and, naturally, I consented. Now she dug down in a box, produced it, and asked me to do another like it, or to draw some other pictures. Instead, I gave her the crayons, but she could make but little of them. She would do a whole sketch with a single colour, but would not attempt to reproduce things in their actual tints.

The wind lashed and pounded my poor tents all night, but about sunrise it fell and gave way to a steady downpour of rain. My small tent was still up, but all the guy ropes were slack in spite of the fact that the rain should have tightened them up a little.

We were in a good camp site here, sheltered as much as we could hope to be, but nevertheless we almost decided to move across to the other side of the peninsula so as to be nearer to the diggings. However, there was but little shelter from the wind there and perhaps we were wiser to stay after all, for Bobby promised us no moderation in the rough weather, now that summer was over.

The *Nascopie* was due back at Port Burwell on her second stop by now and arrangements had been made for the motor-boat to come for me as soon as she was sighted. This could be done before she dropped anchor if the weather were good enough to allow the boat to leave the Post as soon as the ship was sighted.

Once or twice we thought we saw her smoke in spite of the wind and so Bobby brought out his telescope for a real trial of its capabilities. He climbed up to a point from which he could see clearly all the way to the hill which stood between his favourite camp site at the Post and the buildings themselves and then lay down carefully, propping the telescope up on a flat stone, using his green knitted woollen tuque to protect it from scratching on the rock.

First he made sure the focus was right and then he directed it on the hill. He didn't just take a look, close it up with a snap, and say the ship wasn't there. That's what most people who are not accustomed to the use of field glasses and telescopes would do, but not Bobby. He lay very still for at least five minutes and watched. There were at least two possibilities in his mind: first, that the ship might make lots of smoke at one minute and almost none at another, so he had to wait for a reasonable time to allow for that contingency; secondly, there was the risk of mistaking drifting cloud for smoke, so he had to wait long enough to get some idea of how much cloud was blowing over the hill-top, in which direction it was travelling, how fast and with what degree of regularity; then, having learned what the clouds were doing, he would have some chance of recognizing any variation from this, which might indicate smoke.

Even when he had looked long and steadily, he would not commit himself to a categorical statement. He merely said that he didn't think the ship was in, as he couldn't see anything that he felt certain was smoke.

Then he slewed round a little and began to search the hillsides of the land a mile and a quarter away across the inlet to the west of us. He would select a definite point and watch the area he had under observation for several minutes. Then he would move to the next field of vision, making sure it overlapped the first, and watch that area for a time. So he went on, till he had covered every square yard of that hillside.

Whether or not Bobby had had experience with telescopes before, I didn't find out, but at any rate he had been competently instructed in their use. Bobby was looking for one thing, and one thing only—movement. On that distant hillside, he might see, perhaps, three brown objects about the size of caribou. Were they indeed caribou, or were they merely boulders of about that size and shape? Nothing would tell him except movement. If they moved closer together or farther apart they were grazing; if they kept still, they might be sleeping or lying down and only observation for a long time, or at intervals, till they moved or failed to move would assure him that they were indeed nothing but boulders.

In the same way, a large white rock might be nothing but a white rock, but if it moved—why, it had signed its own death warrant if Bobby decided that he would shoot it, for it would be no rock, but a bear.

So Bobby tested his new telescope. It took him an hour or more, but he learnt a lot in those sixty minutes. In months and years to come, that simple arrangement of lenses in a brass tube would save Bobby many hours of fruitless hunting and would lead him again and again straight to the quarry which he had sighted while he was still far away.

During the next night the rain stopped and the morning, though still cloudy, was at last fit to work in. We continued our digging in the igloo, finding but little, and both Bobby and Mark were getting a little fed up with the job. They had never met a man who was so insistent on one thing, and they wished he would share a little more in their desire for constant change and variety of occupation.

More than once Bobby, having finished the little section he was working on, would look up and grin.

"*Taima?*" he would ask hopefully.

"*Auka! Tsiro.*" I would answer, trying to get over the idea of "Not yet, but soon."

Mark, always less dependable and more easily bored, would lay down his shovel or his trowel, beg a cigarette, and wander off without explanation or apology.

One fine afternoon, for we did have an occasional clear day, after a morning's steady work, I felt that a holiday would restore their spirits, especially if it were unexpected.

Suddenly, with no warning, I threw down my trowel and, in as well-simulated a tone of surprise as I could muster, I called aloud.

"Bobby!"

Bobby grunted and looked up.

"*Oodlume* Sunday!" I said.

"*Auka. Ikpukshak* Sunday."

He was quite right, of course, and I know perfectly well that yesterday had been Sunday. Nevertheless, I insisted that this was Sunday, and then he got what I was driving at.

He struck his forehead. He wrinkled his face in astonishment at his own stupidity. He agreed, firmly and with a beaming smile, that this was indeed Sunday and we certainly should not work any more. All the way back to camp he laughed at our stupidity in being tricked into working on a Sunday when we might have been amusing ourselves in a hundred pleasant ways.

Arriving at camp, we put Jenny through the same elaborate farce. Bobby, Mark and I all argued with her, insisting that this was Sunday, a day of rest. Determined to set us right, she went into her tent and, with a serious face, brought out a calendar printed in syllabic script which helps the Christianized Eskimo to keep track of Sundays.

She pointed to the day. It was Monday. We pointed to the previous day. No, Jenny wouldn't believe us, till we pointed out that it had been raining the day before, that it was not raining now and that, for us at any rate, this was going to be Sunday. We were going for a long walk, a Sunday walk, but if she was still convinced that this was Monday, why, of course, she couldn't come.

At last she tumbled.

"*Oodlume* Sunday!" she agreed, with conviction and off we started.

Jenny, unlike her white sisters, didn't find it necessary to change her shoes, or her stockings, or her suit, or renew her make-up, or put on a hat. She just said "*Namut?*" meaning "Where to?" and off we went.

That was one of the finest walks we ever had. There were so many things to see, so many things to talk about.

We came to a shallow lake, not warm by any means, but we all took off our boots and waded about in it, gradually stripping off more and more till we were all splashing about and having the first real bath we had had for a long time.

Then we lay about on the grass, keeping carefully out of the chilly wind, and dried off. That was, perhaps, the third day that summer warm enough for sun-bathing, and it was certainly the last. After a little time, we got dressed again and continued our walk.

Jenny was just behind me, for we were more or less in Indian file, and every now and then I felt her toe touch my heel as she over-reached me in her stride. At first I thought nothing of it, but it had never happened before, and now she did it so frequently that I turned round with a grin to see what was going on. Jenny grinned cheerfully back at me, but made no comment, so I assumed it had been accidental after all, but in a moment it began again and I could hear Bobby chuckling.

Again I turned round, and this time I stopped.

"Look," said Bobby. "Walk like this! Then she won't do it any more."

Bobby walked a few steps with his toes very much turned in and his heels out, with an absurd hobbling gait.

Jenny blushed, pretended to hit him, and giggled.

We took the trail again, but now I walked according to Bobby's formula. Jenny smacked me for my rudeness, if that was what it was, and never trod on my heels again. I never got to the bottom of this business, but suspect that there was some bawly innuendo beyond my command of the language. To my sorrow, I forgot to ask Ernie Lyall about it later.

Now the weather seemed to have taken a turn for the better and the next day I was able to go on with work in

" We saw the smoke of the Nascopie "

" There was a large group of people waiting for the Nascopie "

the igloo. Bobby announced that he had no meat in his tent, so I sent him off to get some.

He started out in his kayak, his harpoon on the deck in front of him, the barrel of his rifle protruding from the cockpit. He paddled off down the waters of Tunnus-saksuk Inlet, the sunlight glinting yellow on his paddle blades. Now the left, now the right, they rose and fell with clocklike regularity. Alternately high and low, the double-bladed paddle looked for all the world like a propeller. No wonder the old Norsemen described them in the sagas as being like windmills.

I went over to the igloo and, just about lunch-time when I was getting ready to go back to camp, I saw Bobby coming over towards me.

"What did you shoot?" I asked.

"*Nanook*," he answered.

"Why, you told me only yesterday that there are no bears around here any more."

"True, there are no more bears here any more. But I got one. Come down to the kayak and I'll show you."

So we walked down to the beach together and there, floating in the clear sea water by the side of the kayak, was a white bear skin. The glistening fur shone and twinkled in the water, taking on a green tint where it had sunk deepest, yellow rather than white where it was out of the water.

Bobby grasped it by one corner and dragged it up on the smooth, shelving rocks on which we stood. He threw it well up beyond the reach of the tide. We laid it out straight and I went over to my tent for a tape. Seven foot six, from nose to tail.

Bobby picked up his boat-hook and, reaching inside the kayak, he dragged out a fore quarter, then a hind quarter, then half the back. Now he turned about and started pulling pieces of bear from the aft section of the kayak. The other two quarters appeared, the other half of the back and, in due course, the head, all of which were laid up on the rocks near the skin.

The intestines had been discarded, but the rest of the internal organs were all there and made yet another section of the bear to be pulled out of the kayak, which seemed to yield up treasure after treasure as though it were Aladdin's cave, till there must have been several hundred pounds of meat piled up.

The liver Bobby had cut up and left behind, so that his dogs could not get at it. All Eskimos are firmly convinced that the polar bear's liver, as well as that of the bearded seal, is poisonous to man and dog, and they never eat it or allow the dogs to have it. Whether it actually is poisonous, always or occasionally, is a matter which is still in dispute and a number of scientists have done some research work on the problem, without any very definite results so far. One opinion is that the liver contains so much vitamin C that it is actually dangerous, except in very small quantities.

Jenny picked up the heart and sliced it open with her ulu to see if there were any parasites inside. There were none in this case, but Bobby told me that worms are often found and that the people never eat it, if the worms are in it.

Now the kayak was empty and Bobby prepared to draw it up on the rocks and wash it, but before doing so he lifted a dozen cod-fish from the little deck before the cockpit. These, he explained, he had caught before he shot the bear.

We all sat by the bear, examining his feet and his teeth, his fur and all about him. His feet were rough and hard underneath and Bobby said that indicated he had been spending his time on land, living on roots, berries, lemmings, and so on. If he had been in the water most of the time, the soles of his feet would have been soft and tender. To confirm this, Bobby said, there had been blueberries in his stomach.

Little Jimmy sat with us, playing contentedly. He had found a new toy, nothing other than the dead bear's windpipe. When he pressed on the lungs, some little air remained inside them and was squeezed out, making a curious growling noise as though in protest.

Jimmy jumped with astonishment and we all laughed at his fright. Then Jimmy laughed too, and, not to be outdone, shouted down the windpipe. Again a slight noise when he pressed on the lungs. This was fun! He could make the bear talk to him. Jimmy enjoyed this somewhat macabre conversation to the full and yelled lustily into the cold, dank lungs which now could only whisper their replies, turning the windpipe alternately to his mouth and ear as though it were a primitive telephone.

Bobby was full of the story of his shooting of the bear. He was paddling along, he told us, not expecting anything but seals, when he saw a white object in the water ahead of him. He knew that bears were infrequent so close to the Post (here he grinned at me), and to his own winter home but, nevertheless, he knew by the size and shape of this thing that it must be the head of a polar bear.

He paddled swiftly over and, sure enough, a bear it was, swimming with the tide, strong and sure. Bobby drew alongside and the bear, unable to do anything but swim his fastest, looked up into Bobby's face to see what manner of danger this might be which so suddenly overtook him.

Bobby got his rifle ready and, as he had to stop paddling for a moment to do so, lost his place beside the swimming bear. Again he seized his paddle to catch up.

At this point, Bobby's sense of drama and, perhaps, his conviction that animals think and feel just as we do, carried him away a little, for he insisted that the bear shielded his head with his left paw and called aloud to Bobby, "Don't shoot!   Don't shoot! "

But shoot him he did, in the left ear, so that the skin should not be marred by a bullet hole, in addition to the unavoidable harpoon wound, for had he not harpooned the bear immediately after shooting it, it might well have sunk and he would probably never have recovered it.

Having secured the bear by the harpoon, he towed it to shore, gutted and flensed it, cut up the carcass, stowed the quarters away in his kayak, and, towing the skin alongside to give it a good wash, returned to camp singing as he paddled.

While we were listening to his tale, most of which I followed easily enough by the help of his dramatization of the whole incident, Jenny was working away at the skin with her ulu, scraping away fat and bits of tissue from the inside, so that it could be dried ready for sale at the Post.

"Would you like to have the skin? " asked Bobby suddenly, turning to me.

"*Marrik!*" I answered.   "Yes, indeed," for I could just see that fine big white skin lying on the floor in my study.

"Good! " said Bobby.   "It's yours."   Jenny grinned and went on working.   It took a long time to scrape it clean but at last it was all done and that evening the big white hide, seven foot six from tip to tail, for I had to measure it again to make sure, was hanging over a rawhide thong stretched between two big boulders. Here it was to hang and dry, as long as the weather permitted.

We were sitting after dinner outside my tent, in the

last warmth of what had been another unusually fine day
and the conversation turned, naturally enough, on bears.

"Are there any lice on bears?" I asked casually.

"No," answered Bobby. "There are lice on seals and
on the walrus, but none on bears."

Suddenly Jenny appeared round the corner of the tent.

"Lice?" she asked, her face glowering. "Who's got
lice? Who says we've got lice?"

Bobby and I laughed loud and long, only increasing
Jenny's irritation. Eventually we sobered enough to tell
her what we had been talking about, but it was quite
evident that she was ready to be insulted at the suggestion that she or any of her family might be lousy.

Next day, at lunch-time, Jenny said she had cooked
some of the bear-meat and asked me if I would have
some.

Bobby and she both watched my face carefully for
they knew that this was, for me, a new venture in the
field of gastronomy.

"*Ee!*" I answered and, using our polite formula, I
added "*Mikkiuk,*" by which I meant only, "Yes, please,
I'd like a little."

"*Mikkiuk!*" Bobby spat out the word with disgust.
"*Angiuk!*" he shouted, irritated at my apparent reluctance to try the good bear he had provided. "Have a
lot."

When I got my share it was, indeed, a lot. It was
boiled, it was not seasoned, and it was not very thoroughly
cooked. I ate it just the same and it resembled mutton
more than anything else I could remember. Not bad,
but not so good either. Later I had some bear steak,
fried, with my few remaining potatoes and that really
was good.

Little Jimmy came in to see me that evening. He
had often come in when his elders were there, but they

seldom included him in the conversation and there were so many things that small boys were not allowed to touch, that he seldom stayed long in so uninteresting a place.

This time he poked his head in and grinned. I told him to come in and sit down. Carefully he untied the strings that held the flap of the tent shut, for the wind was strong and cold again, and then, once inside, he tried to tie them up again. He fumbled with the strings, twisting his tongue about, but the knot was quite beyond his youthful fingers. However, he persisted and at last got them to stay fastened in some sort of fashion and then he came sedately over and sat down in my folding camp chair.

This chair was a perpetual source of delight to all my visitors. I had to show them how it folded up and then allow them to discover how comfortable it is. The brightly striped canvas soon took on a grimy, greasy look as a result of the constant polishing it received from soiled clothes of wool, blanket cloth, seal skin and what-not, a griminess which will probably last as long as the chair itself.

Barely had Jimmy seated himself, proud of at last monopolizing the *kablunah's* attention, when our *tête-à-tête* was interrupted by Jenny, much amused by the knots which she recognized as Jimmy's. She sought medical advice and assistance. Her bowels, she explained bluntly, no longer functioned as they should.

" Not to-day? " I asked.

" *Auka.*"

" Nor yesterday? "

" *Auka.*"

" Nor *ikpukshani,* the day before? "

" *Auka.*"

That was three days. I counted out three laxative

pills and saw that she downed them. Three days—three pills; not the conventional method of prescribing perhaps, but I was informed later that it worked.

Things had been quiet in the medical sphere for a few days, till Lily came in again complaining that her remaining eye was giving her more pain and that she could no longer see to sew with it. I examined it as well as I could with a pocket lens and there appeared to be a growth of some sort on it, far beyond my knowledge of ophthalmology. She had been using a folk remedy of her own which, she professed, gave her some relief. It was to bathe her eye with the juice which clams squirted out from their shells! I had seen her down on the beach, gathering shellfish at low tide, but I had supposed that she was getting them for a meal.

"Yes," she said. "We did eat them, but I wanted their water for my eye too."

There was nothing I could do for her, of course, except to recommend that she see the doctor at the Post. I told Bobby this should be done and he agreed, saying that as we needed some supplies anyway, he would take her in to Port Burwell the next day.

This meant taking Mark along for crew, Lily as passenger, and little Jimmy was to go along with his mother.

Jenny and I would be left alone in camp.

Chapter XVI

THE LAST IGLOO

THE igloo which looked so old proved to be somewhat of a disappointment after all, for there was very little in it. At one time it had been a commodious enough building, and we could see no reason why it had been used so little, if that was the explanation of the paucity of artifacts in it; at any rate it was the best reason we could suggest.

The house was well situated. It had what a real estate agent would describe as a magnificent view of the Strait. The occupants could see everything that was going on in the water only a few yards away and they could scramble down the hill to the shore quickly enough, into their waiting kayaks and off in pursuit of a seal or a grampus.

Often enough it may have been a grampus, for McLelan Strait seems to be a highway for these huge beasts. It may be that I am wrong in calling them grampuses, but I never was able to find out precisely what they were and zoologists have not been able to help me very much either; they seem to incline to the opinion that the "grampuses" were some kind of dolphin, or a white whale. But then, I knew that much about it already!

Nearly every day while we were working on the igloos we would hear one as he came along, stemming the fierce tide which sweeps through the passageway. Always they seemed to swim against the tide, never with it.

It seems funny to say that we would hear them, but nevertheless that was the way in which we knew they, or it, for we seldom saw more than one at a time in the straits, was coming. At first we would hardly be aware of it, then we would hear it more distinctly and suddenly we would realize that we had already heard it two or three times in the previous few minutes, but then it had been just below the threshold of consciousness.

Then we would hear it again, quite clearly this time. It was like a long and heavy sigh. *Phee-ough!* Then there would be silence for perhaps a minute, and we'd hear it again, louder this time. PHEE-OOOUGH!

We'd all look at each other without saying a word. A little grin, perhaps, but nobody said anything. It was almost uncanny this daily visit from a stately creature who lived his own and self-sufficient life in a world so completely remote from ours. I felt, and so did the Eskimos I feel sure, that here was something different, something that was difficult to express, that here was something impossible to comprehend.

Still silent, we would lay down the tools we had been working with and race across the knoll until we stood on top, right above the water, from where we could see a long way up and down the Strait. Sometimes Bobby would grab up his rifle and take a pot shot at the grampus as he passed, but he never hit one. Nobody seemed sorry that he had missed, not even Bobby I believe.

Down the Strait, still some distance off, we would see a puff of vapour rise into the air. There he was! We could see the dark mass of his head as he broke the surface of the water to breathe, then the graceful curve of his back as he sounded again, down below the surface, out of the waves and out of the sight of any possible enemies, though what enemies he might have save the fierce killer whales I cannot imagine. Or was he a killer whale himself?

Then he would break surface again, often enough right opposite where we were standing. We could see the water darken as he came near the top, then his head and the vent through which he expelled the spent air compressed in his lungs. Up would shoot a column of spray and water vapour, more conspicuous on cold days when it condensed in the air.

PHEE-OOOUGH!

Then he would swim on a few feet, the breathing vent still open while he inhaled a supply of fresh oxygen, then down once more, curving slowly and majestically out of sight.

That would be all. We would start to turn away, back to the igloo, but even as we turned our eyes would follow his course and, a short time later, as we left the top of the hill, we would hear him again.

Phee-ough!

And then once more, far off in the distance.

I often think of McLelan Strait, and its deep green waters, the floating ice that races through it on the tide, the harsh bare rocks that line its sides, and always I see swimming along, the grampus of the passageway. Daily, I feel sure, he goes on his way, busy with his own affairs, conducting himself with the dignity and confidence which go with such a bulk as his.

No doubt the old people, the Tunnits, had seen his ancestors go through the same channel in the same way, they had heard his approaching sighs, and hurried down to the water's edge to harpoon him if they could, for there's an awful lot of good dog feed in one grampus.

It was on the first of September that we really did see the smoke of the *Nascopie* off to the north-west of us.

Jenny and I were alone in the camp, for Bobby had gone off with Mark and Lily to ask the doctor to look at her eye. We were working away on the last igloo we should have time to excavate that season and kept glancing in the direction of the Post. We saw the smoke clearly enough without glasses and knew that the motor-boat would come for us, for the weather was clear and the sea calm.

The previous night had been quite uneventful. Jenny had brought me something to eat at the usual time and had sat about chatting while I ate it. We spoke of this and that, of the *Nascopie's* coming again soon, of Mark's boil, of Lily's eye, and other matters of the sort.

Jenny again expressed her dismay at the proportion of grey hairs in my head and tried once more to pull them all out. I had read that an ancient form of torture was to pull out the victim's hairs one by one, the theory being that the pain, trifling at first, grew worse and worse with each jerk, till it grew quite unendurable. Well, perhaps so, but it certainly didn't work in my case. Now and then she got two or three at once, which was less pleasant, but the continual pulling of single hairs was rather soothing than otherwise. I don't know how many she got that evening, but it must have been dozens.

At last she tired of this and it became quite obviously time for bed.

"I'm going to be alone to-night," she commented casually.

"*Ee!*" I answered.

Somehow that seemed to leave things still up in the air. I reached for an English-Eskimo dictionary which generally lay on the table, and looked up the word "*frightened*" or the nearest equivalent.

"*Sivuravok?*" I asked, with an air of concern.

Jenny snorted with contempt.

"*Auka!*" she retorted, and flounced out of the tent.

It was half-past eleven the next morning when we heard the purring of the motor-boat and then two rifle shots, one right after the other, as a signal for us to come back to camp, in case we hadn't heard the boat. We were already on our way, however, and left immediately without waiting for anything to eat when Bobby informed us that the ship would sail again that afternoon.

Jenny, however, a woman first and an Eskimo only second, had found time to put on her best dress and her cleanest duffle parka with the bright embroidery and braid. Soon we came alongside the ship, her black sides towering high above us, and a line of curious faces peered down at us from over the ship's rail. Jenny looked up and, suddenly, she was overcome with shyness. She covered her face with her hands and crouched low in the bottom of the boat, as far down as she could get, presenting only a well-rounded back and stern to the onlookers. She explained to us later that she was embarrassed at so many white men at once. All of them, she felt sure, had been staring at her.

I was still dressed in sealskin boots and a parka. Sealskin boots are not the source of the world's sweetest aromas and the duffle of my parka was stained with the mud of more than one igloo, but just the same I was invited to the Major's cabin later that afternoon, and I had tea with him, and the Doctor, and a Member of Parliament. It felt a little strange, though it was only a few weeks before that we had made up the same foursome in the same cabin!

Things were all pretty much of a rush. There were letters from home, and a parcel which would have to wait till later to be opened. There were provisions to get from Mr. Reid, the chief steward, not forgetting some fresh bread. Never before had I known how good fresh bread is!

Then arrangements for a radio message outside, to assure Ruth that her husband still lived in health and virtue, and a visit to the store at the Post to get some oil for my rifle, some pork and beans, and a bottle of ketchup.

And then, back to camp!

Somehow, it was almost a relief to get away from the ship.

I had not been waiting for her with any great impatience, though her coming was a sort of half-way mark in the summer's work, but I had never dreamed that I should be glad to get away from her only a few hours after boarding her.

Yet, it was definitely with a sense of relief that we all got back into our boat. Lily was with us, her eye just as it was, for the doctor had reported, as indeed I had feared he would, that there was nothing he could do for her in the circumstances. He had not been able to hold out any hope of improvement either.

And here was Mark, leaving his beloved Emily once more, after a grand and hilarious dance the night before.

Davidee was with us too, for he had to take the boat back to the Post.

And little Jimmy was there with a new toy Bobby had bought for him at the store.

We were all glad to be back on our own. Bobby was master of his little tribe and even the *kablunah* deferred to him as the ruler in all matters in which his judgment and knowledge were superior. All the others were his own family and his rule was unquestioned, save only Davidee who had charge of the motor-boat and was not a permanent member of the group.

It was getting towards dusk when we reached the

camp. We had a good run down. We stopped to pick up a fine piece of driftwood, and we met the grampus on his way to somewhere or other. Bobby took three shots at him for luck, but apparently none of them took effect, for the big beast steamed magnificently on, marking each quarter-mile with a watery, spouted, mile-post. The sun was setting red and round over towards Akpatok Island and we were all very happy, glad to be with our own people and away from the ship which, we all agreed with Jenny, had far too many white men on her.

When we came alongside the little shelf of rock which we used as a dock we began to unload our newly acquired goods at once, so that Davidee might begin his run back immediately. Then it was we discovered that Bobby had forgotten the box of stuff from the store, with the oil, the pork and beans, and the ketchup. Evidently the distractions of the big city were too much for him, for he had assured me that he put the stuff on board himself.

We all slept well that night. It was clear and frosty, and the Northern Lights played their majestic organ music in the velvety black sky. Great curtains, green, gold, white and red, swept and rippled; long white streamers, like searchlights, shot from the zenith and began to revolve slowly like a gigantic cog-wheel. Then, clear and distinct as a bell, the honk of high, invisible geese, heading south to avoid the long cold Arctic winter which was so soon to begin.

Later, in my sleep, I was disturbed by a low, far-off moan. Again, the same moaning sound, and I awoke a little more fully. I turned on my flashlight and looked at my watch. Four o'clock. The *Nascopie* was whistling an *au revoir*, as she turned north on the second half of her annual patrol, north, and still farther north, along the length of Baffin Island, the third largest island there is, past Bylot and Devon, till she reached Craig Harbour in Ellesmere Island, the farthest north of the Mounted Police Posts then open in the eastern Arctic.

That meant I had just about two weeks left, for I should have to return to the Post a few days before the ship was expected there on her last call, which was to be on the 22nd of September. This was to avoid getting caught by bad weather and also to give me time to get all specimens and equipment securely packed for the long trip back to Ottawa.

To our surprise the calm weather of the last day or two continued. There was a drizzle of light, persistent rain, and the little inlet behind camp was filled with quilts and comforters of fog, above which the tip of the mast on Bobby's sailboat showed dimly. Still it was quite fine enough to work on the igloo and we returned to it with renewed vigour now that the ship was off our minds and out of the way.

The lower culture layer we had half expected to find in the first of our two igloos here had proved a myth, more or less, and we were satisfied that there was nothing more of importance to be found, so we decided to turn to another.

Not far off were three saucer-shaped depressions which Bobby admitted he had never noticed before. They might be old igloos, he agreed, but he wasn't at all sure. Nor did he show any particular eagerness to find out. The fact of the matter was that Bobby was getting a bit tired of the job. It had been fun for a while and he had taken the work in the gay, picnic spirit in which the Eskimos meet most of their undertakings, but by now he had had enough. More than enough, in fact.

More than once in the last few days he had told me that soon he must go for caribou and to get a supply of wood for the coming winter and it was evident that he

was anxious to start on this autumn expedition as
soon as he could.

I told him that we had still two weeks to work here
and that if we were not sure whether these depressions
were igloo ruins or not, the best thing to do was to get
busy and find out.

Bobby was mad! I could see that well enough. He
scowled at me and grumbled something or other, sent
Mark off to get the shovels and a crowbar, and tore
viciously into the turf. I pretended not to notice these
symptoms, feeling sure that an hour's digging would
sweat the bad humour out of him, which it did, sure
enough.

Under the turf we found a confused tangle of rocks
with masses of dried oil and blubber all through them.
There were no signs of a definite structure, no walls
or entrance tunnels, no sleeping platforms, no tables for
the lamp or places for seal-meat. These certainly had
never been houses.

"*Netchek*," said Bobby, adapting his language to my
understanding. "Seals."

These then were places where seals, caught in a season
of plenty, probably in late autumn, had been cached for
future use. The carcasses had been frozen and then
put beneath the rocks, which had been piled over them to
keep the meat safe from foxes and other predators, who,
otherwise, would soon have made off with it.

On several occasions I had noticed a well-marked trail
which led up from the beach near the igloo we had just
abandoned to the top of the hill and inland in the
general direction of Bobby's winter house. Trails are
common enough when they lead from one end of a more
or less permanent settlement to the other, but this trail
was different in a way which I found it hard to define.

We were sitting having a smoke after our exertions

on the three seal caches and the trail was right in front of us. I called Bobby's attention to it and he grinned with pleasure that I should have noticed it.

"I made it!" he exclaimed, and thumped his chest.

"You? What for?"

He explained that this was the trail by which he dragged his seals from the water's edge back to his house in the winter time. So many years had he done so, so often had he followed the same route, that even through the snow an effect had been produced which was still to be seen.

His father, too, Bobby admitted, had used the same trail for it was the easiest way up the side of the hill, and perhaps many generations before them had made use of the self-same pathway.

Now the question arose as to which of the remaining igloos we should select for our last excavation. So far we had established the fact that the Button Islands had been occupied in recent times, for we had found specimens of both European and Eskimo origin, and no signs of any earlier occupation. We had discovered that our first igloo at the McLelan Strait site was occupied by people of the present-day culture. So far, we had not seen any houses which had been lived in or built by the people of the old Cape Dorset culture, and that was what I was looking for. That there might well be such houses near by was fairly evident for, scattered here and there on the surface, I had found a number of specimens which were undoubtedly Dorset.

We went round from one of the old house ruins to another, noted the height of the walls and the colour of the grass on them. Some appeared much fresher than others, but none of them seemed to be very old. At the end of the little village opposite from where we had been working was a large double igloo; one, that is, in which a

P

dividing wall ran down the middle of a more or less circular structure. In one side of the depression was the huge, bony skull of a whale.

This, Bobby said, was older than any of the other houses. I tried to find out what made him think so, but he didn't seem to have any very good explanation. Perhaps it had been a tradition among the people living there when he was a small boy.

True enough, it did look old in some ways, but even before we started to work on it I could see ends of roof timbers sticking out of the soil near the wall, and the entrance passage was solidly built and still in fair condition. However, it looked more promising than any of the others, so we determined to stake our last chance on it.

We moved all the tools over from the one we had just finished and from the three seal caches, took a few preliminary photographs, and left the actual beginning of operations for the next morning.

That evening Bobby made some more dog traces of bearded-seal skin. He obtained long thongs by making a helical cut in a cylinder of hide and then stretched them tightly from one large boulder to another.

It was just the right place for such a job and he told me he always made use of these same boulders when making skin line. At one point stood a pair of them, heavy, shoulder high, and only a couple of feet apart. Some thirty feet away was another one, more or less spindly in architecture, with a sharp point sticking straight up. Bobby looked his line round this point and carried both ends back to the double boulders. Here he made use of his harpoon shaft, wrapping the ends of the line round it and thus making a sort of extemporized pulley, for by rolling the shaft he was able to increase the tension of the line.

He twisted and turned at the shaft till the line was as tight as he could get it, and then he worked along it carefully with a sharp knife, trimming out all irregularities in thickness, scraping away any hair that might be left on it, and reducing it to perfectly even width and thickness. He worked quickly, but with great care, for a clumsy stroke would see the thong weakened if not ruined. Every now and then as it went on stretching under the tension, he would go back and give the harpoon shaft another twist, and then continue his trimming and scraping.

He pondered some time as to whether he should leave it out all night. He had left his other dogs at the Post, so there was only Sammy, the white dog, to consider. He might chew it up and spoil the whole thing, but that could be looked after by tying Sammy up. Then there was the weather to take into account. For some hours now the barometer had been dropping and Bobby predicted that we should have much wind again soon.

"*Anore amisiut!*" he announced, staring up at the clouds with a weather-wise eye. "Much wind."

He said it would come from the south-west, and pointed in that direction. Sure enough, high above us, the clouds were scudding along, drawn out in long, swishing mares' tails. Towards evening a few pale stars were seen and flickering, weak Northern Lights.

However, to my great satisfaction, the next day broke fine and clear. Every day counted now and delays from bad weather were the last thing I wanted. Bobby decided that he would help me get the sod and top rubbish off the new igloo and that he would then take the sailboat and Mark and run up to the Post to get the box of supplies he had left behind a couple of days before.

So we all started to work, ripping off the turf and laying bare the remains of the roof timbers. The wood

did look surprisingly fresh and my heart sank more than
once as I examined them. Surely this could never be a
really old igloo; the wood was firm, there were even bits
of leather and feathers to be seen lying about here and
there just below the turf.

By lunch-time we had the roof timbers out of the
way, the debris of sod from the roof shovelled out, and
we were ready to go ahead with the layer-by-layer examination of the deposits in the igloo itself. We had begun
in the half where the whale skull was not, as this was
the larger half and more promising looking.

Bobby looked about him with satisfaction in a good
morning's work. Now, he felt, he could start off for the
Post with a clear conscience.

"*Taima?*" he asked.

"*Taima!*" I agreed, and we put down our tools and
went off to lunch.

Bobby and Mark left right afterwards, with just
enough breeze to carry them easily before the wind, right
up McLelan Strait to the Post, the tide helping them on.
They were to bring the stuff they had forgotten, a few
other odds and ends which I detailed in a letter to the
post manager, and also, if they could get it, something
for Lily's eye, for it was paining her a good deal now
and she bathed it often in clam juice.

All that afternoon, warm and sunny, Jenny and I
worked on the new igloo. It proved richer than anything
we had found yet and we were chattering away as we
dug. I was working on the side nearest the south, where
the walls never got any direct sunlight and it was not
long before I ran into frozen soil.

"*Hwach!*" I ejaculated, and scraped at the icy layer
with my trowel.

"*Kwak,*" corrected Jenny. "You said it as the old
people do, *hwach.*"

I made some joking remark about being fairly old myself, using the word *pitohak* for old. Now *pitohak* does mean old, right enough, but it means an old thing, not an old person, and she was much amused at my selection of the wrong word. "*Pitohak igvit*," she would say, "You're an old thing," chuckling with delight at the incongruity of the phrase, which was more apparent to her than to me.

Later, when I found a toy sled runner, I held it up for her to see, saying *komatik mikkiuk, venek, imaha* by which I was trying to express the idea "sled, small, once was, perhaps." It was an awful example of a white man's efforts to speak Eskimo, in all probability nobody but my immediate "family" would have understood what I was trying to get at, but it brought forth great praise from Jenny. She looked at me with an expression of mingled surprise and admiration.

"Why," she said, "you'll soon be an Eskimo yourself, for you talk almost as we do."

Chapter XVII

A FORMAL VISIT

THAT evening was perhaps one of the most quiet and peaceful that I remember spending in the North. The sun was still warm and there was only the gentlest of breezes, but a sharp nip in the air reminded one of the scarlet and gold of autumn farther south. Up here winter would not long be delayed now.

After getting something to eat, Jenny and I and little Jimmy went for a walk, leaving Lily huddled over the stove nursing her aching eye and puffing on her short, black pipe. No, she said, she didn't want to go for a walk.

More or less from force of habit we turned in the direction of the igloo where we had been working all day. Passing by it, we came to the little stream which trickles down past Bobby's winter house and empties into a small cove. Here we saw a school of fish, swimming leisurely in the quiet water, their dorsal fins just cutting the surface. Presumably there was something in the inflowing fresh water which held an interest for them, either physical or gastronomic, though I could not see that they were feeding. They were thick-packed in their little school, reminding me of the salmon in the rivers of British Columbia when they came upstream to spawn.

The grampus came puffing along as we stood there, full steam ahead, turning neither to the right nor to the left. Jenny and I grinned silently. Never have I known an anonymous animal to have so much personality and character as that beast had.

We wandered about for half an hour or so, listening to little Jimmy's exclamations as he found rare "specimens" for me, and then strolled back to camp. I lit my Coleman lamp and started work on my notes and collections, and I could hear Jenny working at something or other just outside her tent. As she worked, she sang. Not the slow and doleful hymn tunes they have learned at the missions, but the old native songs with their strange and lovely melodies, haunting yet impossible to retain in one's memory. She had a fine, clear voice, true and pure in tone, and sang without self-consciousness. Whether she knew that I could hear her or not, I couldn't tell, but she was certainly not singing for my benefit, but quite unaffectedly.

Many of the native Eskimo melodies are very beautiful and nearly all the people have a great love of singing, often composing their own music and their own words. Nearly everybody sings as a matter of course, though some, naturally enough, are better singers than others. Many of their melodies have been recorded by the phonograph and transcribed into our notation, revealing a wealth of first-class folk music where one might hardly suspect it to exist.

Later on, Jenny and Jimmy came in to see what I was up to, as they so often did. Jenny pre-empted my folding chair and little Jimmy found a place on one of the various boxes which lined the walls. I gave him some blank paper and coloured crayons, but he couldn't get much out of them.

Jenny noted a can of condensed milk near the stove and, using it as a starting point, began to ask me things about "my land," as she put it. It was difficult to answer

her, both because of the language and because it meant
dealing with things quite unknown to her.

Bobby had once asked me where oranges came from
and I had pointed to a diminutive blueberry bush, saying
that they grew on plants something like that but much
taller, as high as the mast on his sailboat.

"Pretty big berry!" commented Bobby, and it was
hard to tell whether he believed me or not.

Now Jenny wanted to know about milk.

"Where do you get *imuk*?" she asked.

"From an animal something like a caribou, but with
smaller antlers," I explained and tried to draw a cow
for her. Now cows are not easy for me to draw, but I
managed to outline the head and body, four legs, the
horns and tail and, most important of all, the arrangements for getting at the milk.

Jenny was quite familiar with the fact that female
mammals give milk, but it had apparently never been
quite clear to her that this stuff in the cans was actually
the milk of some animal, an animal not altogether unlike
a caribou. She didn't relish the idea, for the Eskimo do
not milk the caribou as the Lapps milk the reindeer and
the notion of milk being obtained from such a bizarre
source did seem a bit repulsive.

"*Peeungnetuk!*" she exclaimed, meaning "Bad" or
at any rate, "Not so good."

Bobby and Mark were still away when night fell and
we realized that they couldn't get back till the next day.
Probably there was a dance going on and Mark was once
more with his beloved Emily. Davidee was having a lot
more active competition now that Mark was closer to the
Post.

It was nearly eleven the next morning before they
turned up. The wind had risen during their absence and
was dead in their teeth on their return trip. Bobby had

to tack back and forth across the narrow water and it was surprising to see what good time he made in spite of all the delay imposed by this method of sailing. He had the oil for my guns, both of which needed it, for steel and iron rust quickly in this moist, salt air; he had some soothing ointment for Lily, pork and beans, ketchup and various other things. Big dance last night, just as we had suspected.

We spent the whole day working on the igloo and collected an imposing number of specimens. At last we seemed to have struck a really good culture layer, as a reward for all our previous disappointments.

The wind rose steadily and the barometer fell just as fast. Before the day was over it was blowing as hard as it had the week before and once more we had to look to the guy ropes of our tents, place new stones in the path of the dragging anchors and, in general, prepare for rough weather.

Jenny found a rip in the side of my smaller tent and got to work at once sewing it up, which was difficult enough with the wind striving to snatch the cloth from her grasp. However, I held it firmly while she sewed and we got it done eventually. Two or three other places looked as if they were getting ready to let go and I hoped that it would last through the night.

It didn't! It was early morning, long before daybreak, that I awoke with a wet and heavy mass across my face. Strong bonds held me firmly pinned in my sleeping bag and I had to wriggle and struggle for some time before I could get to the door, untie the strings and crawl out.

I tried to put the tent up again by myself, but it was obviously hopeless, so I called to Bobby to come and give me a hand with it. In a few minutes, Jenny and he and Mark tumbled out and the four of us managed to get it up again. While we were doing this Bobby's own tent came down with a run, and my flashlight revealed the shapes of Lily and little Jimmy burrowing their way out of their cocoon.

After a while we got that up again too, and settled down to sleep the rest of the night. My tent slapped and banged, talking loudly the whole night through, but I was used to that by now and, in a few minutes, was blissfully unconscious. It stood till daylight and then, as I was at breakfast in the other tent, down it came again. This time we left it there till evening, thereby saving ourselves a lot of work, for the wind blew harder and harder every hour.

That night the Northern Lights took a new form, a powerful beam shooting up to the zenith from the east, like a strong searchlight. From the west another similar beam was projected, but not so bright as the first. Soon these broke up into a number of fingers pointing up from the northern horizon and they flickered off and on as though some giant switchboard were concealed behind the distant hills.

The wind had dropped a little by morning, though still very strong, and my diary records the unusual combination of wind and fog: "Heavy fog this morning with a 'Scotch mist' and the wind still too high to leave the tents."

I spent the morning numbering and listing the specimens we had collected, now up to over four hundred, wrapping them in little squares of newspaper with their numbered slips enclosed, and packing them away in empty boxes in which my supplies had come. Some were too wet to pack, especially those of wood or bone, and these were left in the shelter of the tent to dry. This they did but slowly, in spite of the warmth of the stove, for the air was always heavily laden with moisture.

Mark came in to watch me working, or perhaps just to sit with me, while he busied himself carving a model of an Eskimo lamp in soft stone. He was using a pocket-knife with a red plastic handle and carrying in inlaid metal letters the magical words "Old Stock Ale."

His little lamp was not very well made, but he presented it to me, after bumming another package of cigarettes. Apparently these levies were beginning to gnaw on his conscience and he felt that he had better make some sort of a return.

He said wistfully that he wished he could go "outside" with me when the ship came to take me away. It would be an interesting experience for him, no doubt, but a somewhat expensive one for me, for he would have to stay almost a year till the annual voyage of the *Nascopie* could carry him home again, he would have practically nothing to occupy his time, nobody of his own language to speak to for he knows barely half a dozen words of English and has not the remotest knowledge of our culture or customs.

There have been several stories of the adventures of Eskimos who did go outside for a time. Some of them are merely amusing, others tell of various misadventures, sickness and death. One boy, who visited Winnipeg, took all the strange sights very much for granted till he saw a man riding a bicycle. Then he collapsed on the curb, convulsed with laughter at this supremely ridiculous sight.

So our last days passed. Work on the igloo continued whenever the weather would allow it and the number of specimens mounted rapidly.

One day, prowling along the side of the little brook, I came across what was, I soon realized, an old rubbish dump. Here were several quite good Cape Dorset specimens, fragments of polished nephrite or jade, some curious rubbing stones presumably used for polishing the jade, implements chipped from quartzite, and at least one of the peculiar curved knives which are typical of the Dorset culture.

This led me to search for other deposits of rubbish and soon I found several, along the side of the brook and also in the lee of the hillock on which the village stood. Farther round the hill, towards the north, was a much larger rubbish heap and here the quartzite specimens were very numerous. There were long thin flakes with parallel sides, there were chipped points, knives and scrapers. A few specimens were chipped from chert rather than quartzite and some of these had been rubbed smooth on their edges or sides, another characteristic of the Dorset culture.

Here, clearly enough, there had been an old settlement of the Cape Dorset people, and they had been followed by the modern Eskimos who had occupied the same site for the same reason, the continuous supply of seals, summer and winter.

It was a big day. Bobby rejoiced with me, for he had long hoped that I would at last find Dorset material, the things made by the old Tunnits as he called them, in large enough numbers to be sure they had been left there as the result of a definite settlement, rather than just an odd one here and there as we had done so far. Pleased as he was, he could not share all my enthusiasm, for he didn't realize that this was the first Dorset site to be worked by an archæologist who knew that it *was* a Dorset deposit that he was digging.

It was McLelan Strait that I had to thank for my success and the open water caused by the swirling currents. This feature of the place was commented on by Dr. Robert Bell, apparently the first scientist to visit the village, in 1877. He says:

The locality is called Nunaingok by the Eskimo, which means "the hidden place." . . . It is situated on an alluvial flat, extending between the two branches of the strait. . . . On top of a bank of sandy earth are the remains of an old Eskimo village. The roofs of most of the underground houses have fallen in, leaving only the circular pits. Some of these have become partially filled up, showing great antiquity. A few of the newest of them had been inhabited within a year. Some Eskimo encamped in the vicinity informed us, through our interpreter, that this had once been a comparatively populous village, and a resort of their people as far back as their traditions extend. It is their custom to live in the underground houses from the commencement of winter, some time in November till January, after which they leave them and spend the rest of the winter in igloos or snow houses. The water in the north branch of McLelan's Strait, they informed us, is open all winter at this point, and is much frequented by seals, which afford them a reliable supply of food. These animals they kill, either from their kayaks or by spearing them from hiding-places which they have built of stones on every ledge and point of rock past which the seals are accustomed to swim. Great numbers of bones of seals, walruses, reindeer, foxes, hares, birds, etc., lie scattered about on the surface and mixed with the earth around the old dwellings. The remains of stone pots and implements near others of European manufacture showed a transition from a barbarous to a civilized condition.

Of course, I took all the photographs I could as the work progressed. I thought I was taking photographs, rather, but I was all unaware of one sad fact.

On returning from one of our walks I had been somewhat laden down with rock specimens and Mark politely volunteered to carry my camera. I knew that he was most curious as to how it worked, but thought nothing of it. He slung the strap over his shoulder and I forgot all about his having it. When we got back to camp I went to my tent and he to his, and it was not till an hour or so later that he came over to give me the camera. I thanked him and laid it aside without looking at it.

When next I used it, however, it became evident that things were not as they should be. It was a Kodak 3A and I found that the two springs which hold the back in place had both been bent, evidently in an attempt to open it. However, the front slid out all right, the bellows extended with no difficulty and I went ahead making exposures. It was not till the films were developed, weeks later, that I discovered that they were all badly out of focus, because the bridle in which the lens is mounted had been bent out of line. Clearly, Mark had been doing a little research work during that hour between our return to camp and his giving me back the camera.

This was the day of a phenomenon which puzzled all of us. We were hard at work in the igloo, each of us crouched over his own section of the work, scraping away, showing each other specially interesting finds and pausing now and then for a stretch and a smoke. Suddenly there was a loud and prolonged roaring noise, which seemed to come from right above our heads. It sounded almost as though a flock of huge birds was just above us.

We all stood up and looked about. There was not a thing out of the ordinary to be seen. We scrambled out of the igloo and ran to the top of the mound. Still nothing. We looked at each other in search of an explanation, but nobody could offer one. Was it an aeroplane? Hardly, for the sound was not sustained enough for that. Was it a Torngat, one of those spirits which inhabit the mountains a few miles to the south of us, whose name they bear? Possibly, Bobby admitted, but added that he had never heard a Torngat flying and couldn't be sure.

Then I remembered a somewhat similar sound which I had heard in Switzerland years ago. Could it be an avalanche, far away? Bobby considered this for a moment. It might be, he agreed, though it was late in the year for one. He had seen them himself, on a small scale, coming down the hillside to the east of us, and they had indeed made a very loud noise, and not unlike what we had just heard. That might be it, but we still didn't know.

That evening I dug up an old copy of *The Illustrated London News* which I had noticed in my wrapping paper where there was an excellent series of photographs of avalanches. I called Bobby over and he was immensely interested and pleased to see them. I tried to explain where away Switzerland might lie, for it was there that the photographs had been taken, but it was tough going. We dropped that phase of it without any very satisfactory conclusion being reached.

The topic exhausted, Bobby turned the pages over one by one, looking at the pictures. Many of them meant nothing to him, but he was much interested in a fine picture of a lion. I explained that the animal was much like a very large cat.

"*Ee*," he agreed, as though he knew all about lions already, and added in perfectly good German "*Löwe*." Evidently the Rev. Mr. Waldmann of the Moravian Mission had made some excursions into the natural history of foreign lands with his pupils.

Jimmy was the hero of the day, not long after this, when he shot his first game—a seagull. In theory this showed that he had now attained the status of a hunter, able to secure his own livelihood, able to seek a woman of his own. Not that anybody thought these things really had come to pass, least of all Jimmy, but rather that his first success as a hunter was a token, an earnest, of greater triumphs to come.

Bobby was immensely proud and showed me the dead bird. He and Jimmy had been down at the water's edge just near the shelving rocks where the boat lay while we landed our supplies and equipment. Here Bobby had been seated, his legs spread wide, with Jimmy seated between them. In this position the little boy could hold the ·22 rifle while his father guided his aim and steadied his arms. It was Jimmy who actually pulled the trigger.

They had been shooting in this way for some time at any target which offered itself, a chip of driftwood or some floating seaweed, when an incautious gull came to rest only a short distance away. "It must have been a deaf one," Bobby suggested with a laugh, as the noise they had been making didn't seem to alarm it.

Jimmy saw the gull and loaded the rifle again eagerly. He settled himself firmly between his father's thighs and arms to take a good aim. Bobby told me he could feel the trembling of the little arms as Jimmy strove to control his excitement. He held his breath, squeezed the trigger, fired. The seagull, as Bobby showed me in pantomime, simply closed its eyes peacefully and turned over on its side in the water. Not a kick, not a splash, and Jimmy had got his first game.

Bobby shouted aloud for us all to come and examine the proof of his son's prowess. Now he was a real hunter. Assuming the casual nonchalance of those to whom these are everyday occurrences, Bobby launched his kayak and held it still while the great hunter stretched himself on the after deck. They paddled out to the dead bird and little Jimmy himself lifted his trophy from the water. It was indeed a great occasion. Lily and Jenny praised him aloud and he was so overcome that he nearly broke into unmanly tears.

As custom decreed, the new hunter presented his first game to other people in the camp, thus symbolizing the hope that he would always have so much meat that he could afford to give it away to others. The seagull was boiled till reasonably tender and Bobby gave portions to all of us to eat. I chewed mine and got it down all right, thus partaking of the symbolical feast, but it was not a very tasty dish.

I was rather glad to get out of Bobby's tent on this particular occasion, for there was an appalling stench of long-dead fish about. Jenny was aware of this and also knew that the white man is less broke to stinks than the Eskimo. She apologized for the odours and pointed out the offenders. She could smell it just as well as I could, but apparently she minded it less.

But Jimmy, in spite of his new-found honours, was still but a small boy. While sitting in their tent on a sunny afternoon, a tiny perforation in the canvas threw a small spot of sunlight on the back of my hand. I turned my hand over so that the light fell on my palm and then called Jimmy's attention to it. Moving my hand a trifle seemed to make the spot move as though it were alive, and he tried to pick it up with his little fingers. I shut my fist and he tried to pry it open to get at that bright spot which must surely still be in there. I let him succeed and so arranged matters that, when my hand opened again, there was the spot of sunlight still on my palm.

Jimmy was greatly intrigued. For a long time he attempted to solve this problem and even when I held his hand so that the light fell on his palm it was all a mystery and far beyond him. Then Jenny showed him the tiny hole in the tent wall, blocked it so that the sun no longer

Q

shone through, took her finger away and again let the spot fall in his hand. Still no understanding, no realization that it was the sunlight he had to deal with though she tried to explain to him in his own language.

We found a curious little wooden scoop while working in the igloo one day. It was a tiny thing, nothing more than a toy apparently, holding perhaps as much as a large teaspoon. I showed it to Bobby and Jenny, who were working near me, and we puzzled as to what it could have been made for. Nobody had any suggestion which was very convincing, till an idea occurred to me.

I reminded Bobby that, in the old days, people used to give a newly killed seal a drink of fresh water as a ritual expression of their sense of compunction and regret at the necessity that made them deprive the seal of its life and as a mark of respect to Sedna, the goddess who lives at the bottom of the sea and has dominion over all seals.

Bobby knew all about this, for his father had told him of it, and once, when he was on a trip many miles to the south on the east coast of Ungava Bay, he had actually seen it done by some Eskimos with a rather more primitive form of culture than his own and not much influenced by the missions. But, he said, they had not used a little scoop like that for the purpose, and so we were no further ahead in our speculations. In all probability it was a child's toy, or had been made as a model to put on a grave and, in that case, had never been made for actual use at all.

We had visitors on one of the few fine days that were left to us. We were just finishing lunch when Jimmy's sharp eyes detected three kayaks approaching from the north-west. He called out to us and Bobby's telescope and my field glasses were soon trained on them. They were three men who had apparently noticed our tents when on a seal hunt. Now they were paddling over towards us.

I looked at Jenny.

"Tea?" I asked.

"*Ee*," she assented and went off to her tent to make sure the water was hot and tea ready for our visitors.

Bobby and his family also retired inside their tent as though quite unaware anyone was coming. I went into mine and kept out of sight, watching their arrival without showing myself.

The tide was low and the three kayakers paddled their craft up on the low shingly beach, near the boulders between which Bobby stretched his lines for dog traces. They didn't look up at the tents, or talk to each other, but pulled their kayaks out of the water quietly and slowly. There was a deliberation in all their movements which let us know that they were aware that they were being watched.

The kayaks safely disposed of, each man reached inside his craft and brought out a gift. One had an *ekaluk*, a fine big Arctic char, and the others each a good piece of seal-meat. Each laid his present on the deck of his kayak, then they washed their hands carefully to get rid of the blood and grease from the seal-meat and have them clean for shaking hands with their hosts.

At last they were ready to present themselves. Each man took his gift in his left hand, so that his right should be free. Sedately they advanced up the beach, two towards Bobby's tent and one towards mine, each conscious that he was doing the correct thing in the approved way, following the rules of etiquette laid down by their forefathers and still observed among themselves, no matter how much the new teachings may have broken them down near the trading stations.

It was a pleasant thing to see and one that will remain

in my memory long after other things have been forgotten.

My visitor entered my tent without any warning or ceremony and deposited the fish with a smile on a box near my gasoline stove. I said *"Nagomek!"* and he had no trouble in understanding that I was thanking him.

"Netchek?" I enquired politely, which he could take to be a question as to whether they were after seals or as to whether they had been successful.

"Ee," he agreed, which didn't advance matters much.

"Tea?" I enquired, and held a cup towards him.

This time he understood readily enough and nodded and smiled politely, saying *"Nago"* in his turn.

I poured out tea for us both and gave him a cigarette with his. We both lit up and smiled at each other. I gave him a large handful of biscuits, after pointing to the fish, and again thanking him for his gift. These he accepted with thanks and promptly put them in the hood of his parka.

This, he felt, ended his ceremonial visit and we both adjourned to Bobby's tent where the other two were drinking tea and eating bannock. My new acquaintance then produced the biscuits I had just given him, passing them to everybody present including myself, and we all sat round for an hour or so, smoking and talking.

At last our visitors rose to their feet, thanked us again, shook hands ceremoniously all round and paddled away.

"Peeouyuk?" asked Jenny, meaning more or less "Did you enjoy the party?"

"Ee!" I said, and I certainly meant it.

Before they had much contact with white men, the Eskimos used to rub noses on meeting old friends after a protracted absence. This is seldom done now, though I did see it at Pangnirtung on the east coast of Baffin

Island. It is not the vigorous, nose-smashing rubbing that the cartoonist seems to expect, but a gentle approaching of one face to the other, as though they were about to kiss. The noses barely touch, if at all, and there is a gentle intake of breath, as though sniffing. The lips make no contact at all.

Chapter XVIII

LAST DAYS AND FAREWELL

OUR work on the last igloo was practically all finished. It had never been occupied by the Dorset people after all for we found but few of their specimens inside its walls, most of them being on the old rubbish dumps outside, often some distance below the surface.

As a matter of fact, I have never seen a house which I am sure was built by the Dorsets, a regular structure, that is, with walls built up of stones and provided with sleeping platforms.

On the rubbish heaps near by we found many good Dorset specimens and, had we discovered at the beginning of our stay how plentiful they were there, instead of towards the end, we might well have collected many more.

I had made my sketch map of the site, measuring the distances from one igloo to another and the distance from each to the sea, the height above sea level of the various control points and their relative positions.

Then I packed my remaining supplies in boxes for transportation back to the ship, after giving Jenny what she felt she could use, which was a good deal. The bear skin which Bobby had given me had been pegged out to dry, and we had had such fine weather during the last few days that it could now be rolled up and tied in a bundle. Bobby remarked that the Company used to pay twenty dollars each for them, but hastened to assure me that he didn't want me to pay him for this one, that it was a present.

Jenny went out in the afternoon with the ·22 and shot some fish as they were swimming near the surface. She fried slices of one of them for my evening meal with a little bacon. There were tea biscuits, which she was now becoming quite expert at making, and even jelly, which was not as great a success as it might have been, for she had made it with cold water and it was somewhat, well—granular.

All that evening I worked at my specimens, now some six hundred, numbering, wrapping and packing, till I had them all done. Then there were last notes to write up, the map to check over, and my diary to bring up to date. It was pretty late that night before I turned in.

When we were at lunch the next day we heard a motor-boat cross the inlet. We thought at first that they were coming to get us, even though we had not expected them till the next day. Then we supposed it was somebody else, and that they had not seen us. We were just about to fire two shots to attract their attention when we saw the bows of the boat turn in our direction.

It proved to be a group of Hudson's Bay Company apprentices, who were waiting at Port Burwell for the *Nascopie*, which was to take them outside. They were out in the hope of getting a seal, but when they saw our tents they decided to come over.

I took them to the diggings, after a mug-up, and showed them what we had been doing. We picked up a few more surface specimens, and I collected a couple of skulls from a grave which I had marked down some days previously.

As the work was finished, and the boat actually there,

it was decided to return to Port Burwell at once, rather than have the boat come back for me the next day. So we struck the tents and folded them away in their canvas bags, we moved all our stuff down to the boat and, once more, loaded it on board.

At last all was in readiness. Actually it had not taken long, for we were on our way soon after three in the afternoon and got to the Post about five, with a steady rain falling and our camp site blacked out behind us by a heavy shower.

On the way in, we met once more our old friend, the grampus of McLelan Strait. There was great excitement and some of the boys tried to shoot it. He sounded at once each time he was fired at and we would all keep a good look-out to spot him as soon as he came up again. We would cry out "*Tukko! Tukko!*" or "Look! Look!" as our habit made us, and off the boat would go in a new direction to head him. Once more, for he must bear a charmed life, he swam off unharmed as far as any of us could discover.

There was a large group of people waiting for the *Nascopie*, that is to say about ten altogether. There was among them the wife of a missionary whom we had brought in only the year before. There were, too, Hudson's Bay Company staff going outside after a term of service, and one or two Royal Canadian Mounted Police constables also being relieved.

There was a marvellous dance in the warehouse that night. There was never any need of an excuse for holding a dance, and this time it was because Bobby and his family had returned with their *kablunah* and also because Bobby was going away again immediately on his autumn quest for caribou. He got four, I learned, when I saw him again the following year.

This time both my Coleman lanterns were requisitioned to light the dance floor, for Bobby was much impressed by the radiant light and wanted to show off to the others the modern comforts he had enjoyed in camp. Then, too, we had a drum, something that at least some missionaries do not approve of. It was not the regulation Eskimo drum, made of a narrow wooden hoop over which a piece of thin caribou hide is stretched, but merely an empty tin can which had once held some of my provisions. Nevertheless, it made a good hearty boom and helped the concertina along considerably.

After the dance, a few of us reassembled in the living quarters and were treated to a curious drink compounded, who shall say how or from what, by the Doctor. All that one could say in its favour was that it was a drink, but it added to the festive atmosphere and helped celebrate my return to civilization.

Next morning, Bobby got his pay and all his accumulated wages were placed to his credit with the Company. I called him and Mark and Jenny and Lily into the warehouse and opened up some packages which had been lying there waiting for me.

First I got out a pair of hip-length rubber boots which I had brought along with me. They were not new by any means, though still serviceable, and I hardly thought it worth taking them back with me.

These I placed to one side and a large, thick, dark red sweater beside them. I turned to Bobby, who had been watching all this, and asked him which he would prefer. Without hesitation he selected the rubber boots, and was delighted to get them. This left the red sweater for Mark, but there was no sign of disappointment, and he took it with many a "*Nago!*"

For Jenny and Lily I had some bead necklaces, some other bits of jewellery and, to their great delight, for each a compact complete with mirror, powder and puff. They chuckled and giggled with excitement and Jenny at any rate certainly knew what a compact was for and appreciated its function in life.

For little Jimmy there was a football, something that at first he was almost afraid of, but within a few minutes he had collected a scratch team from heaven alone knows where and a vigorous, if ill-regulated, game was in progress over half Killinek Island.

They all seemed pleased with their presents, and we all said "*Aksunai!*" to each other again and again, and hoped that I could come back again the next year and see them all, and then we'd go to another place Bobby knew of where the houses really were old and we'd find everything the Tunnits had ever made.

Little Jimmy was rounded up, his football tucked under his arm, and Bobby and all my family sailed away, down the harbour and round the point and out of my sight.

There was one addition to the family. It was Emily. Bobby had said something about it at the dance the night before, but I hadn't quite gathered what he had meant. Now there was no doubt, and the beaming face of proprietorship on Mark, and the pride with which he wore his new red sweater, were both delightful to see. At last, boy gets girl, even in the land of the Eskimos.

It had been like a visit to another planet, this journey to the North, over the rounded shoulder of the world, along the rugged coasts and the ice-packed seas which stretch away to the Pole itself.

It's a new world, not only physically, but also mentally. Physically, because it's a world stripped to the bare essentials, rock and water. There is little else. Vegetation, that decent covering of Mother Earth, which we take so for granted, is unimportant or, at least, inconspicuous, often invisible at any distance over a hundred yards. There is the land, harsh and bare, with its ponds and streams; there is the sea, with its rocks and islands; and there is nothing else, save ice on the sea, and snow and glaciers on the land.

It's a new world mentally too. Danger and courage are the key notes. Danger, because one lives perforce close to the elemental forces of nature. Though it is seldom mentioned, there is danger in one's daily travels —danger from storms at sea, from rocks awash, from tide-rips and swirling currents, from cranky boats and balky motors, from wounded bears. There is danger from winter blizzards, from the penetrating frost, from starvation, from accidents which, often trivial in themselves, may leave one, helpless, to die only a few miles from mankind and safety.

And there is courage, courage none the less heroic because it is never spoken of by the men who live down North. Courage to face dangers known and unknown, courage which leads men to venture as a daily habit, as a matter of course, where we, used to the shields and safeguards of civilization, would go only under the spur of the most desperate necessity.

And this new world has its own inhabitants, the Eskimos. *Innuit*, they call themselves, "the people." Not *the* people, superior to other folk, but rather the *people* as distinct from the seals, the caribou, and the bears which share their land with them.

As a love of this land grows on him who comes to know it, so, in even greater measure, does a love of its people. Many virtues are theirs, their vices are few. They have in them those qualities which make of Man an admirable being. They are kindly, they are courageous, they are generous and hospitable, and, in spite of the dangers and hardships which they face daily, they are happy, cheerful and genial. When there is work to be done, it is done; no talk, no wrangling, no argument as to how or why; the work is *done*, quickly, quietly, efficiently.

One leaves the North with a keen sense of regret, with a feeling that one is giving up something that is very good and returning to a life which, whatever else it may be, is not quite so good; a life where problems are more numerous and more complex, but where the stakes are of less value, the decisions of less importance, the gains less desirable.

In years to come, those who have seen the North will never forget it. There will be a hankering to return to a land in which life somehow seems closer to the ideal life, that mythical life of the Golden Age, when the Earth was young and the spirit of Man was the spirit of Youth.

APPENDIX

NOT all my readers are familiar with the technical aspects of archæology or with the details of the migrations of various Eskimo groups. For this reason, no stress has been laid on the scientific results of my visit to the Button Islands and McLelan Straits. For those, on the other hand, who do take an interest in such matters, a short note follows.

Three distinct Eskimo cultures are recognized in the eastern Arctic: the Dorset, the Thule, and the Modern. Of these, the Dorset is the oldest and, at least in some districts, it is overlapped by the Thule culture. Where the Thule people came from and when they invaded the area occupied by the Dorsets, we do not know. Last to appear on the scene was the Modern culture, that of the Eskimos who now live in the eastern Arctic and their immediate ancestors. Their culture merges imperceptibly with the Thule and there is no chronological marker separating them.

The outstanding difference between the Dorset culture on the one hand, and the Thule and Modern on the other, is that the Dorset people made extensive use of stone implements chipped from chert or quartzite and never made tools by grinding slivers of slate into shape as did the Thule and Modern people, who not only used this technique extensively, but who seldom used the chipping technique.

The Dorset culture is quite definitely Eskimo, but there are curious features about it. For instance, there is no evidence that these people made use of dogs as draught animals as the Eskimo of to-day do, for we have found none of the ivory buckles and swivels which are used with dog harness and no models of dogs, or of sleds, none of the accessories used with sleds. Neither have we evidence that they were acquainted with the kayak, since no kayak equipment, very common in the Thule and Modern cultures, has been found. The bow-drill, an almost essential tool for the Eskimo of to-day, was also unknown and all their holes are either slotted or reamed out with a hand-drill.

Their houses, too, offer a problem. Not yet has any ruined igloo been found which is indisputably of the Dorset culture. The year after I worked with One-eyed Bobby and his family, I dug an old site near Cape Wolstenholme at the south-west corner of Hudson Strait, and found a number of saucer-shaped depressions in a dry, gravelly ridge. There were no signs of a stone wall or of a roof, nothing but shallow pits, though they were undoubtedly house sites.

The purpose of my expedition was to try to find out more about these three cultures, particularly the Dorset. Excavation of the two igloos on the Button Islands revealed only Modern material. There were, in addition to objects of Eskimo origin, pieces of iron and chinaware, clearly indicating intercourse with white men, probably whalers, numbers of whom have visited this part of the world since 1750. Some of the specimens found might have been considered to be Thule if they had not been associated with Modern material. There were no Dorset specimens at all.

At McLelan Strait, I found some Modern material on the surface and in the excavation of the two igloos. Lying about, also on the surface, were numbers of chipped stone implements of the Dorset culture, made from a translucent grey quartzite. I found a good many more of them in a row of small rubbish heaps round the seaward edge of the promontory on which the old village stands. Here, too, were a few pieces of polished nephrite, typical of the Dorset culture, and some curved knives chipped from chert, also Dorset.

This was the first time that Dorset material had been excavated by any archæologist, knowing it to be Dorset. Most previous specimens, including those on which the very existence of the Dorset as a distinct cultural entity was predicated, were picked up and brought in by Eskimos with only a hazy account of the conditions under which they were collected. Their discovery *in situ*, with no Thule material present, clinched the argument as to whether the Dorset might not be merely an aberrant form of the Thule.

To the Reader

If you are a subscriber to a
circulating library you may
like to be advised of our
new books as and when
published. A card to us
giving name and address
will ensure that you receive
these particulars regularly

MUSEUM PRESS LIMITED
33 Woburn Place London
W.C.I